Ancient Magick for Today's Witch Series

PROTECTION MAGICK

MONIQUE JOINER SIEDLAK

Shamanic Magick © Copyright 2020 Monique Joiner Siedlak

ISBN 978-1-950378-26-5 (Paperback)
ISBN 978-1-961362-20-8 (Hardback)
ISBN 978-1-950378-25-8 (eBook)

All rights reserved

The content contained within this book may not be reproduced, duplicated or transmitted without direct written permission from the author or the publisher.

Under no circumstances will any blame or legal responsibility be held against the publisher, or author, for any damages, reparation, or monetary loss due to the information contained within this book, either directly or indirectly.

Legal Notice

This book is copyright protected. It is only for personal use. You cannot amend, distribute, sell, use, quote or paraphrase any part, or the content within this book, without the consent of the author or publisher.

Disclaimer Notice

Please note the information contained within this document is for educational and entertainment purposes only. All effort has been executed to present accurate, up to date, reliable, complete information. No warranties of any kind are declared or implied. Readers acknowledge that the author is not engaged in the rendering of legal, financial, medical or professional advice. The content within this book has been derived from various sources. Please consult a licensed professional before attempting any techniques outlined in this book.

By reading this document, the reader agrees that under no circumstances is the author responsible for any losses, direct or indirect, that are incurred as a result of the use of the information contained within this document, including, but not limited to, errors, omissions, or inaccuracies.

Cover Design by MJS

Cover Images by MidJourney

Published by Oshun Publications

www.oshunpublications.com

Ancient Magick for Today's Witch Series

The *Ancient Magick for Today's Witch Series* is a series for modern witches to explore ancient magick, covering Celtic, Gypsy, and Crystal magic, among others. It offers practical advice on spells, rituals, and enchantments for today's use, incorporating natural energies and spiritual connections. With insights into Shamanism, Wicca, and more, it helps readers enhance their magickal journey, offering paths to protection, prosperity, and spiritual growth by combining ancient wisdom with contemporary practice.

Wiccan Basics
Candle Magick
Wiccan Spells
Love Spells
Abundance Spells
Herb Magick
Moon Magick
Creating Your Own Spells
Gypsy Magic
Protection Magick
Celtic Magick

Shamanic Magick
Crystal Magic
Sacred Spaces
Solitary Witchcraft
Novice Witch's Guide

MONIQUE JOINER SIEDLAK

GET UPDATES, FREEBIES & GIVEAWAYS

JOIN MY NEWSLETTER

MOJOSIEDLAK.COM/MOONLIGHT-MUSINGS

Contents

Introduction	xiii
1. What Is Shamanism?	1
2. The Shamanic Consciousness and Worldview	5
3. Shamanic Territories	13
4. Bringing the Shamanic Dimension into Your Daily Life	21
5. The Shamanic Journey	33
6. Psycho-Spiritual Work Between the Worlds	43
7. The Power and Beauty of Ceremony and Ritual	49
8. Dancing with Spirits	57
9. The Medicine Wheel	65
10. Spirit, Soul, and the Sacred in Nature	71
11. Embedded in the Cycle of Life	81
12. Sacred Medicinal Plants	89
13. Shamanic Work in the Dream World	103
Conclusion	109
References	115
About the Author	121
More Books by Monique	123
Don't Miss Out	127

Introduction

If you're reading this book, chances are you're searching for purpose or looking for ways to live a more meaningful life. You're not alone in this journey—a lot of people go through a period of uncertainty. Stressors at school, work, or home often lead us to question our current way of life.

Right now, you might feel like you're trapped in a small boat in the middle of the open sea with no land in sight. Maybe you've come across a fork in the road, and you don't know which direction to take. Perhaps you're in a phase of transition—a succession of changes has made you feel untethered and unsure. No matter what your current situation is, the principles of shamanism can help you find clarity and give you the gift of peace.

This book will take you on a worthwhile adventure. We will talk about shamanism as a religion that connects us to nature, the cosmos, and our higher selves. We will look at the foundations of the religion and how its traditional principles, practices, and tools can help us in the modern world.

We will start our discussion with the basics of shamanism. In the first chapter of this book, we will answer two central

Introduction

questions that will help us gain insight into what the religion is. One, what is shamanism? And two, where did it originate?

From there, we will talk about the shamanic consciousness, territories, dimension, and journey; the psycho-spiritual work of shamans and the power and beauty of ceremonies and rituals; dance, the medicine wheel, and sacred plants as essential tools in shamanic work; the sanctity of nature and the cycle of life; and the dream world and its significance in shamanism.

There's so much to learn from this book. Hopefully, by the end of it, you will learn how to apply the guiding principles of shamanism in your life so that you can be free from the troubles and woes of the modern world. I want you to release yourself from the chains that bind you—choose freedom by embracing the shamanic way of life.

ONE

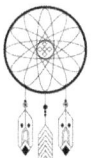

What Is Shamanism?

SOME SAY THAT SHAMANISM IS THE EARLIEST FORM OF religion. Though considered a religion, shamanism does not believe in a Supreme Being. It does not follow a strict set of rules like the Ten Commandments of the Jews or the Five Pillars of Islam. At its core, shamanism is the belief that there is "a spiritual connection that exists between everyone and everything in the universe" (Turner, 2004). It believes in the collective experience. You can say that shamanism is a way of life that allows you to expand and explore beyond your physical limitations. To be able to connect with what you can't see, you need to set your soul free.

The origins of shamanism are not clear, although most scholars agree that it has existed since prehistoric times. Native and aboriginal tribes all around the world had "elders" and "spiritual leaders" who can be compared to modern-day shamans. Rock art, hieroglyphs, and other prehistoric relics also point to the existence of shamanism or, at the very least, practices that highly resemble it. Cave drawings in Europe, for example, showcase figures that bear a resemblance to the human form and that are surrounded by tools and objects that were used for rituals (Harvey & Wallis, 2016; Hoppál, 2013).

The etymology of the word "shaman" is often attributed to Tungusian languages in Eastern Siberia. But the Tungusian word "saman" actually derives from the Chinese word "ša-men," which derives from the Pali word "samana," which derives from the Sanskrit word "çramana," which refers to a person who practices extreme self-discipline and abstinence for religious reasons or the pursuit of a higher consciousness (Laufer, 1917).

The term "shaman" did not surface until the 17th century. A Dutch merchant named Evert Ysbrants Ides was tasked by the Russian Czar Peter the Great to make contact with Chinese Emperor Kangxi. His mission was to establish trade relations and to initiate talks about finalizing the border between the two nations. During his journey, he encountered someone he described as a "diabolical artist" from a Tungusic tribe in Siberia. He called this person a shaman in the report that he sent back to Russia. However, Adam Brand, the secretary of the expedition, who was also of Dutch origin, was the first to use shaman in a brief report that he wrote about the journey (Bremmer, 2016).

Some will argue that shamanism is the religion of uncivilized hunters and gatherers or that it doesn't belong in modern society. However, most literature about shamanism is biased with Eurocentric ideologies that discredit it as an illegitimate religion (Harvey & Wallis, 2016). As we all know, Western Europe is responsible for spreading Christianity as a religion throughout the world. From the exile of the apostle Paul in Greece to the Crusades to overseas expeditions, Europeans used Christianity to exert political power over other countries around the world (Pelikan, 2005).

As a religion, shamanism revolves heavily around spirituality. A shaman will learn how to connect with the spirit world through an altered state of consciousness. Traditionally, the ritual aims to benefit not only the shaman but also the social group he/she belongs in. Prehistoric tribes relied on shamanism to explain phenomena they couldn't understand. Predating science, they used nature to find meaning. They connected with spirits in nature and power animals, among others, to give guidance to their communities (Tributsch, 2018). This is why you will find a lot of natural elements in shamanism even today.

Modern shamanism, or neo-shamanism, still involves a lot of the traditional concepts of shamanism. A shaman must be able to enter an altered state of consciousness so he/she can embark on a spiritual journey. Basic skills and tools, such as ceremonies and dances, are also still in play.

For the purposes of our discussion, we will define a shaman as one who has the ability to enter and exit an altered state of consciousness voluntarily, travel to realms beyond the physical, and interact with spiritual entities. Furthermore, a shaman will use these abilities to benefit the greater good.

This does not mean that you cannot apply shamanic concepts to improve your self and well-being. But your intentions must not be selfish if you want to practice shamanism. How will self-improvement help you help others? This is a question that you'll hopefully get to answer as you read this book.

TWO

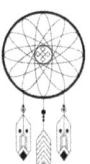

The Shamanic Consciousness and Worldview

HISTORICALLY, THE PRIMARY ROLE OF SHAMANS WAS TO provide spiritual and psychological guidance to their community. They were also considered to be the first physicians and psychotherapists of humankind. During rituals and ceremonies, shamans voluntarily entered a controlled altered state of consciousness to be able to communicate with (and sometimes incorporate) spirits. Also, they may have had out-of-body experiences to visit the spirit realm, travel through time, or explore remote parts of the world (Krippner, 2007; Walsh, 2001).

There are several ways that a person can be selected to become a shaman, including the following:

- inheritance (being born in a family of shamans),
- bodily signs (having an additional digit, albinism, or an unusual birthmark),
- uncommon actions (having seizures or exhibiting traits and behavior typical to the opposite gender),
- strange experiences (lucid dreaming or having out-of-body experiences),
- survival of a near-fatal disease,

- dreams or daytime reveries (Krippner, 2007).

In a lot of shamanic tribes, the last qualifier is of utmost importance. It was a common belief that the spirits chose a person to become a shaman if they appeared to her or him in a dream. In other words, an individual is personally called by the spirits. Because this way of selection is considered special, we will focus on the shaman's dream, calling, and initiation to have a better understanding of the shamanic consciousness and worldview.

The Shaman's Dream: Calling and Initiation

Once a shaman reaches adolescence or adulthood, they should receive a calling that marks the beginning of their shamanic journey. This calling will sometimes come in the form of a dream or a daytime reverie. Once they receive the calling, they undergo training before they are initiated. Some training has lasted for years, like the shaman Igjugarjuk, who was left in an igloo for 30 years with little food and water to sustain him. Fasting, sexual abstinence, and extreme exertion and physical stress were standard in the training process. These activities were intended to make the shaman's mind and body stronger. A shaman will also be forced to face their fears and improve their skills, including endurance, patience, and concentration (De Rios & Winkelman; 1989; Walsh, 1994; Walsh, 2001).

During training, candidates will have a deeper connection with the universe. They must learn how to travel in the spirit realm. They get familiar with its inhabitants and their powers. At the same time, a shaman should figure out whether to battle or befriend these spirits, how to control them, and how they could help the shaman in his or her work. This is the time that a shaman should build a relationship with the spirits. However, not all training processes are made equal. The training process differed from tribe to tribe, although there were three common aspects in most shamanic training processes: inner teachers, myths, and vision quests (Walsh, 1994).

Inner Teachers

During training, a candidate will learn how to enter an altered state of consciousness and coax helpful spirits to reveal themselves. These spirits will be his or her inner teachers, and their messages "may appear in dreams, daydreams, images, journeys, or visions" (Walsh, 1994).

When it comes to neo-shamanic training, your inner teacher will be the inner voice in your head. You have to cultivate that voice because it will tell you what your body and mind need. Listening to your inner voice can also help you realize the path you need to take. Whenever there is turmoil around you, seek that inner voice, and find the truth it wants to reveal.

Myths

Myths were unique to a specific community. They served four major functions for the tribe as a whole: developmental (maturity and life stages), social (life and relationship), cosmological (cosmos and the role of man), and religious. These were also guiding principles in the shamanic training. A candidate will have to learn the myths of his community. Afterward, build his or her belief system around it. This is very important because a shaman must have a shared belief system with members of the tribe for healing rituals to be more effective (Walsh, 1994).

You don't need to belong to a tribe to be able to build a shamanist belief system in the modern age. However, you have to establish a set of principles to live by. You are respecting people and nature, practicing meditation regularly, developing more meaningful relationships with others, cultivating your creativity. Including seeking peace even amid chaos are just a few examples of the kind of guiding beliefs that will help you grow in your shamanic journey.

Vision Quests

Remember Igjugarjuk, the shaman who stayed in solitude in an ice hut for 30 years? This type of vision quest—or an extended period of solitude, reflection, and fasting—was a normal part of the initiation process. Such a vision quest could last between a few days to several years, depending on the journey the candidate would take. Vision quests were meant to empower the body, mind, and spirit. As a result, the candidate would be able to cultivate self-control, extinguish, and purify one's conflicting desires, and redirect focus away from the outside world and its distractions (Walsh, 1994).

You don't have to follow Igjugarjuk's footsteps to be able to unlock your shamanist potential. But you have to be consistent in your practice. Meditation and fasting should be a regular part of your training.

You may find meditation difficult at the beginning, especially with an untrained mind. It is your mind's instinct to wander from thought to thought without a clear direction or purpose. However, with continuous practice, the inner voice we were talking about earlier will become much more apparent. You will slowly learn to ignore worldly distractions. In time, it will become much simpler to explore your thoughts and to focus on seeking answers through meditation.

Meanwhile, fasting will help you purge unwanted desires. Note that fasting doesn't only apply to food—you can also abstain from other things that you have an unhealthy dependence on. For example, regular "binge-watching" can be impeding your goals. Instead of exercising, meditating, forming bonds with other people, or being productive, you choose to be alone and sedentary. This is the type of solitude that is not good for you.

So try to withhold from this desire when you fast. You can also purge social media addiction, alcohol, smoking and other vices, excessive shopping as a form of retail therapy, and other similar cravings that don't lead to self-improvement through your neo-shamanic training.

Lastly, remember to keep solitude and fasting hand-in-hand with reflection. The only way to truly understand yourself as well as what constitutes your idea of who you are is to reflect on what these practices reveal to you.

The Shaman's Worldview: Hylozoism and Animism

The shaman's worldview can be summarized in two doctrines: hylozoism and animism. Both of these doctrines believe that everything in the universe has a consciousness, but let me be more specific:

Hylozoism is "the belief that all things are instilled with life," while animism is the belief "that every object is invested with a mind or soul" (Walsh, 2014). Mackinnon (2018) further elaborates on the shamanic worldview:

1. All things in the universe possess a spirit;
2. All things in the universe are made of energy;
3. All things in the universe are interconnected;
4. All things in the universe are sacred and always evolving;
5. All things in the universe, even those we can't see, are real.

In other words, shamanism considers the universe, as a whole, to be a living being. You can say that the universe is like a person whose inhabitants are like internal organs that are all interconnected. Each organ has its own function, but they all contribute to the whole. Consequently, all organs are significant because they all perform a specific purpose. Though you can't see all of your organs with your bare eyes, they exist and are real.

Critics would argue that these beliefs are insignificant in the modern age when materialism and consumerism are the norms. People are way less connected and personally dependent on nature. We are not hunters and gatherers anymore. We don't build our shelters with our own hands. We buy our food from the grocery store, our tools from the hardware store, and our clothes from the department store.

Most of you that are reading this book are probably living in an urban landscape. Your homes are stacked on top of one another. Cities are crowded with high-rise condominiums and apartment buildings filled with Ikea furniture. Every season, there's always a new catalog to look forward to.

We are surrounded by roads and buildings made of concrete. We go to work and spend most of the day inside a cubicle. Our jobs revolve around desks and computers; we sit and stare at a screen for hours on end.

We live in an age when traveling means rest and relaxation instead of finding a new place with enough resources to sustain a tribe. We only get a chance to connect with nature during these vacations and getaways, but they only amount to a few days or weeks in a year. Even then, we live in hotels with blackout shades, comfortable beds, air-conditioning, and a pool. Today, our relationship with nature is mostly recreational, not personal.

Materialism and consumerism have created a significant disconnect between us and nature. Critics of shamanism will use this as a reason to denounce the religion. They might say that shamanism is outdated or that it has no place in the modern world.

However, I would argue that this disconnect is the very reason why we should practice shamanism today. The shaman's worldview allows us to rediscover and rebuild our relationship with nature. It also forces us to reevaluate our dependence on material possessions.

You might realize during your training that materialism and consumerism are an enormous part of the reason why you feel lost and unsatisfied. You might be measuring your self-worth by what you have and what more you can own. You might have unconsciously formed an unhealthy habit of comparing your possessions to others'. You might be rewarding yourself with expensive things even though you know that they will never be able to fill the hole in your life. At the end of the day, material things will not give you a sense of purpose—only a vicious cycle of longing, desire, and dissatisfaction.

When you adopt the shaman's worldview, you will learn that nature has everything you need. It will sustain you if you respect it. You will learn to prioritize your basic needs and find happiness in the simplest things. When you commune with nature, it will be easier for you to separate your self-image from your material possessions. The shaman's worldview will also help you find peace and clarity once you've denounced materialism and consumerism and found your way back to nature.

THREE

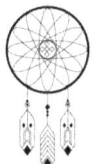

Shamanic Territories

SHAMANIC JOURNEYS ARE NOT RANDOM VOYAGES. ALTHOUGH shamanic rituals, trances, and dances may look chaotic and disorganized to non-believers, shamans follow a general map to access the different shamanic territories. As I mentioned earlier, they undergo extensive training to make their minds stronger so that they can be more receptive to what the spirits want to reveal to them. Part of their training is to familiarize themselves with the different shamanic worlds. To follow the right journey in order to communicate with the spirits.

In this chapter, we will talk about shamanic territories and how shamans are able to traverse in them. Note, however, that although shamans follow a general map, they are still free to wander and to interpret what they find based on the different training aspects that we discussed in the previous chapter.

Gateway to the Spirits

Before we dive into the different shamanic worlds and journeys, there is an important concept that we need to discuss. The axis mundi (also known as the cosmic axis, the center of the world, or the center of the universe) is an idea that appears not only in shamanism but in other cultures and religious beliefs as well.

For instance, mountain peaks are regarded by different peoples as the axis mundi. Locals built shrines at the foot of Mount Fuji in Japan, Mount Kun-Lun in China, and Mount Kailash in Tibet. Mountains are also significant for different religious groups like Mount Sinai and Mount Zion for Jews, Mount Olivet and Mount Calvary for Christians, and Haram esh-Sharif or the Temple Mount for Muslims. At the same time, ancient civilizations like Egyptians, Africans, Mesoamericans, and South Americans built pyramids to mark what they believed to be the center of the world ("Axis Mundi," 2016).

In shamanism, a tree often marks the axis mundi. Some tribes believed that the branches and leaves symbolize the upper world, the trunk symbolizes the middle world, and the roots symbolize the lower world. The cosmic tree was used by the Iroquois in North America, the Mayans in Mesoamerica, and by peoples in India, Persia, Siberia, and Mongolia. Even Christians have a cosmic tree in the Bible. The tree of life, which was planted in the middle of the Garden of Eden. There is also the tree of knowledge from which Adam and Eve ate the fruit. Interestingly, the Christmas tree, though the holiday is Christian, takes root from the Scandinavian pagan cosmic tree (Mackinnon, 2018; Genesis 2:9-3:6, English Standard Version).

We talk about the axis mundi because it serves as a gateway to the spirits. As I mentioned earlier, it represents the connection between the three worlds. Therefore, shamanic journeys begin in the opening presented by the axis mundi.

Shamanic Worlds

The cosmos is divided into three different levels: the lower world, the middle world, and the upper world. Although connected through the axis mundi, they are not linear. The shamanic worlds are not like a three-story house where you can move from one level to another using a simple staircase. Each level doesn't have a specific floor plan that divides the space into individual rooms. Again, we go back to the image of a tree—the lower and upper worlds are like the roots and branches that grow in all directions. These two worlds are the spiritual realms, while the middle world is both physical and spiritual. All three worlds are infinite. It is the shaman's task to find his or her way around these complex maps.

Lower World

Different cultures and religions have different notions of what the lower world (also called the underworld) really is. In some belief systems, the underworld is a place where souls go to be punished after death. In shamanism, the lower world can be home to evil spirits. But it also takes the form of different types of natural landscapes inhabited primarily by the spirits of animals with the addition of the spirits of other natural entities. It can be accessed through the roots of the cosmic tree or any other portal that leads down, including wells, tunnels, and holes in the ground (De Velasco, 2005; Mackinnon, 2018; Serr, 2019c; Siikala, 1987).

The journey to the lower world happens through dreams, visions, and voluntary trances. During the descent, the shaman will have to face challenges that the spirits present to him or her (De Velasco, 2005; Siikala, 1987). According to Mackinnon (2018), these spirit helpers may provide "images, sudden insights, emotional reactions, [and] energetic forces" that make the journey "more instinctual than intellectual." These spirit helpers allow the shaman to discover new information about oneself. In a sense, you can say that the lower world is connected to the human psyche.

Not to mention, shamans also visit the lower world for a myriad of reasons such as:

- To see the future,
- To predict the weather,
- To find lost objects,
- To help lost souls find their way back (which can be part of a healing ritual),

- To guide the soul of a sacrificial animal,
- To guide the souls of the dead to their final resting place (de velasco, 2005; siikala (1987).

In neo-shamanism, the descent to the lower world is primarily concerned with the discovery of self. For instance, if who you are and who you want to be is currently in conflict, you can go on a journey to the lower world to discover how you can reconcile both ideas of yourself. Remember that this realm is connected to the human psyche. Therefore, the lower world can help you learn new things about yourself that may help you in the present or guide you to a destination you wish to reach.

Middle World

In the middle world, the physical and spiritual entities coexist. Five types of spirits inhabit this realm: nature spirits, ancestral spirits, intrusive spirits, nonhuman spirits, and the spirits of those that have passed but are yet to transcend (Serr, 2019a).

Nature spirits in this world are different from those that inhabit the lower world. While animal spirits occupy the latter, a shaman can communicate with the spirits of natural elements that exist within the physical realm in the middle world. These include but are not limited to rocks, plants, trees, mountains, and heavenly bodies (Mackinnon, 2018; Serr, 2019a).

There is a specific risk that comes with a trip to the middle world. It can be dangerous to visit this realm, especially if the shaman is not well trained. Some spirits that are trapped here can be aggressive and hostile. This is because most of the spirits that are unable to transcend have experienced traumatic and violent deaths. A shaman might encounter this kind of spirit in a war zone. He or she might also encounter intrusive spirits in the middle world. Like parasites, these are spirits that feed on your power. If an intrusive spirit attaches itself to a shaman, the shaman might lose some of his/her abilities and have a weakened defense system. An intrusive spirit may further take advantage of these complications, leading to worse consequences for the shaman (Serr, 2019a).

Therefore, a shaman must first train in the lower and upper worlds before treading in this realm. The spirits in the lower and upper worlds are more benevolent or, at the very least, neutral. They can help the shaman develop his or her abilities so that he or she can be prepared when it's time to travel in the middle world.

For a beginner, I highly advise that you avoid the spiritual middle world while you're still developing your shamanic abilities. Think about it this way: You don't learn how to swim in the deep end of the pool, and the middle world is the deep end of the shamanic realms.

Upper World

Though the upper world and the lower world are both spiritual realms, they are very different from each other. First of all, the upper world appears brighter and more colorful than the lower world. It is an ethereal place characterized by pastel colors, crystal structures, and cloud-like scenes where spirits appear in human and angelic forms (Mackinnon, 2018; Woolcott, 2015).

Secondly, while the lower world is instinctual, the upper world is philosophical. Here, a shaman can discover insights that are beyond what the human mind can perceive. This makes the upper world an excellent place to gather information and to seek wisdom. Spirits here are powerful teachers and shamans go back to this realm in order to continue learning and evolving in their practice (Mackinnon, 2018; Serr, 2019b).

To access the upper world, one must find an entry point that's heading up, like the branches of a cosmic tree, a high mountain, or smoke. The shaman must travel in a direction that's higher than where he starts his journey. In most cases, the shaman will know that he has arrived in the upper world when he breaks through a cloud or a cloud-like structure (Serr, 2019b).

In neo-shamanism, the goal of visiting the upper world is to meet your "higher self," i.e., the version of yourself that holds wisdom and learnings from your past experiences. As individuals, we are often short-sighted when it comes to our history. We tend to repeat the mistakes that we have made in the past. Due to the fact we forget the repercussions that our actions bring into our lives. The upper world is where you see the bigger picture.

If the lower world can help you discover new things about yourself, the upper world can help you remember your past selves and the lessons they have taught you. Your higher self, who is both wise and intuitive, can provide insight and guidance in moments when you're unsure of how to proceed. They can also be an origin of inspiration for when you feel lost and unmotivated.

Shamanic Journeys

In my encounter, there are four types of journeys that a shaman can take in order to access the different shamanic worlds: mental, physical, soul, and spiritual.

Mental

A mental journey also requires emotional skills. We engage our thoughts and feelings on this voyage so we can adequately interpret our visions and dreams and then apply them in the real world. In a mental journey, we learn how to plan and think objectively, but we also use our emotions to guide our way. We enter this expedition by finding our center through meditation and relaxation. This journey activates the alpha waves in our brains.

At the beginning of your training, you might find this journey extremely challenging. Your senses can overpower your mind and ruin your concentration. The key is consistent practice, so you can quickly come to a place of calm solitude.

For instance, try mindful breathing. This is just one of the exercises that you can do to hone your skills. With your eyes closed, inhale for seven seconds, hold your breath for four seconds, and then exhale for another seven seconds. While you count your breathing, you should assess your body and how it feels throughout the exercise. Are there points in your body that feel numbness, tightness, or pain? Notice how your chest rises and falls with every breath you take. You can also move your focus from the tips of your toes to the ends of your hair and then back down again, scanning every inch of your body as you breathe. This exercise allows you to practice concentration and reflection so that you can set aside distractions from the physical world.

Physical

A physical journey makes use of our senses—what we can see, hear, feel, taste, and smell. In most, if not all, physical journeys, the shaman is awake and aware of her immediate surroundings, using her senses to interpret signs in order to find any indication of danger or opportunity. This journey activates the beta waves in our brains.

In your practice, you will also need to embark on a physical journey so that you can sharpen your senses and instinct. The skills you will acquire in this voyage will be extremely helpful when you enter the spiritual realms. Your improved sight will help you see your direction more clearly. Your improved hearing will help you better understand the messages coming from the spirits. Your refined instinct will help you in assessing whether a spirit is friendly or hostile. Therefore, don't take these physical journeys for granted. You might be shocked at how beneficial these are in your training.

Soul

Shamans engage their souls when they perform ceremonies and rituals. Although the soul's journey can be voluntary, it can also be unintentional because dreams and visions are part of this journey, and we know by now that they are integral to the shaman's work. This journey activates the theta waves of the brain.

To begin your soul's journey, you may need to perform ceremonies and rituals involving dances and sound, which you will learn more about in the next chapter. At the same time, you should be open to fortuitous images in dreams and visions, which you will get more intuitive about as you progress in your training.

Spiritual

The last shamanic journey you can embark on is spiritual. This is where you can reach enlightenment. You can become one among the cosmos and its inhabitants. During a spiritual journey, the delta waves in your brain are activated, which are usually only engaged when you enter deep sleep. As you awaken from your spiritual journey, you will feel refreshed and rejuvenated. Imagine a fountain being turned on after a period of drought—life, power, and passion will rush through your veins like water as you tap into the ultimate source of energy, the cosmos.

Note, however, that the spiritual journey is accessible only when you reach more advanced stages of your training. Therefore don't get dissuaded if you are unable to embark on a spiritual journey when you begin your practice. It will come to you once you've honed your shamanic abilities, which you can do by giving a lot of attention and putting in a lot of effort into your mental, physical, and soul's journeys.

FOUR

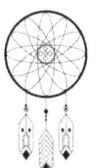

Bringing the Shamanic Dimension into Your Daily Life

ALTERED STATES OF CONSCIOUSNESS ARE INTEGRAL TO shamanism. They allow a shaman to travel to different shamanic worlds and communicate with spirit helpers and inner teachers. Several methodologies enable a shaman to enter an altered state of consciousness. In this chapter, we will talk about these traditional shamanic methodologies and how you can apply them in your neo-shamanic training. We'll begin this discussion by taking a look at the fundamental skills and tools that a shaman needs and then follow that up with actionable steps on how you can bring the shamanic dimension into your daily life.

Basic Skills and Tools

In a cross-cultural examination of different shamanic tribes around the world, Mackinnon (2018) identified a recurring set of basic skills and tools that grants a shaman access to an altered state of consciousness. These include ceremony and ritual; vibrations and sound; movement, dance, and trance-dance; nature; shamanic helpers; power animals; power objects; and spirits, including spirit guides, spirits of ancestors, and spirits of nature.

Ceremony and Ritual

From the perspective of an outsider, shamanic ceremonies and rituals may appear supernatural because they usually involve symbolism that varies by culture. These symbols, as well as their interpretations, can be physical, literal, or metaphorical, depending on how they are used. For example, Korean shamans treated unfulfilled desires by wearing the color red, Mayan shamans used candles in healing rituals, and Cuna shamans recited a myth to facilitate a difficult birth (Rasmussen, 2004). Furthermore, shamanic ceremonies and rituals served different purposes within a single community. For instance, they can be used:

for healing, for rites of passage, for blessings, initiations, dedications, and cleansing, for the shaman's flight and journeys, for giving something back to the Earth, for expressing gratitude and for quests and meaning and purpose (Mackinnon, 2018).

These nuances make shamanic ceremonies and rituals appear otherworldly when taken out of context. But looking at how they served shamanic communities, you can see just how significant they were.

The key takeaway here is that ceremonies and rituals are at the heart of shamanism, and you, as a practitioner of neo-shamanism, will also have to engage in these activities. In Chapter 7, we will discuss how you can perform your own shamanic ceremonies and rituals.

Vibrations and Sound

Vibrations and sound often go side by side with shamanic ceremonies and rituals. They come in the form of drums, songs, chants, and hums. Shamans use vibrations and sounds to drown out worldly distractions so they can prepare for the journey that they are about to take. These tools allow them to focus on the ritual and to call on spiritual entities if need be. Drumming, in particular, can be used to engage different wavelengths of the brain. The rhythm can also be adjusted to match the heartbeat of the shaman. These practices allow the shaman to more easily enter an altered state of consciousness (Mackinnon, 2018).

In addition, some shamanic tribes decorated their drums to represent their cultures and worldviews. The Sámi people in northern Europe, for example, drew figures of gods, humans, animals, and other symbols that the shaman interpreted as a part of a ritual. Shamans also created their own drums and, therefore, could have an intimate connection to their instruments. It is believed that the figures on the face of the drums are like cognitive maps that give others an insight into the inner workings of the shaman's mind (Pentikäinen, 2010).

In neo-shamanism, vibrations and sound are still significant. They can accompany both movement and meditation. During your practice, you can play shamanic drums, songs, chants, and hums through popular music streaming platforms like Spotify.

Movement, Dance, and Trance-Dance

You should remember in Chapter 2 that part of the shaman's worldview is the belief that each and everything in the universe is composed of energy. Through movement, dance, and trance-dance, the shaman's body is stimulated and, as a result, produces energy that taps into the energies surrounding him or her. A shaman might also perform a ceremonial dance in order to embody the spirits that he or she wants to communicate with. Aside from connecting a shaman to energies and spirits, ceremonial dances are also performed as a form of therapy. They give the shaman a safe space to release repressed emotions like unwanted desires, to relieve tension and stress, and to achieve self-actualization (Mackinnon, 2018; Winkelman, 2010).

In Chapter 8, we will further discuss the biopsychosocial benefits of movement, dance, and trance-dance. You will also learn how you can perform contemporary adaptations of traditional shamanist dance rituals.

Nature

We've already talked about the importance of nature in shamanism. It doesn't just exist in the physical world; shamans also see images of nature and natural elements in the spiritual realms.

In contemporary shamanism, communing with nature is a skill that you have to develop. You will realize during your practice that nature has a healing effect on the mind, body, and soul. It can revitalize you during periods of stress, anxiety, and burnout. This is why, if you haven't noticed, a lot of people retreat to nature when they want a break from their busy and exhausting lives. People hike a mountain, go camping, or take vacations to the beach. As human beings, we are creatures of the Earth, and we seek to reconnect with our roots when we are feeling lost or running on low.

The best way to connect with nature is to pursue quiet solitude while in nature. Listen to the rustling leaves, the chirping birds, the blowing wind. What message is nature trying to tell you?

Shamanic Helpers

Shamanic helpers refer to spirits that guide the shaman through different quests. They can be power animals, power objects, and spirits, including spirit guides, spirits of ancestors, and spirits of nature. These spirits exist in the non-physical realms, so the shaman has to call upon them, often through song, if he or she wants their help in performing healing and ceremonial works. Aside from acting as helpers, these spirits can be sources of power, wisdom, and protection (Mackinnon, 2018). We will discuss the different shamanic helpers in more detail in the succeeding sections of this chapter.

For now, what you have to know about shamanic helpers is that they are willing to assist you in achieving your desired results. If you humbly seek their help, they can open doors for you that you didn't even know were available. You need to develop a relationship with your shamanic helpers that is founded on mutual trust and respect. It is not a one-way relationship—you must also give back to your shamanic helpers through thanksgiving and good works that benefit other people.

Power Animals

Have you heard a friend talk about their spirit animal? In contemporary jargon, a spirit animal doesn't have to be an animal per se, but it is a creature that embodies one's personality. The concept of a spirit animal also appears in pop culture. For instance, in J.K. Rowling's Harry Potter book series, witches and wizards would summon their patronuses when they need protection from dementors. Most patronuses take the shape of animals, while dementors are dark, cloaked figures that hover and suck someone's soul. Can you see how these contemporary ideas of spirit animals are founded on shamanist principles?

Shamanic helpers that take the shape of animals are called power animals. They provide assistance, protection, and wisdom both in the physical and spiritual worlds. Shamans seek power animals to guide them in healing and soul retrieval. They can also boost a shaman's creativity, strength, and connection with nature (Mackinnon, 2018).

Power Objects

Power objects take many shapes and forms. Feather bundles, drums, sacred pipes, and stones are just some examples of power objects. These tools can give energy and be recharged if necessary. They are also used in different shamanic rituals, including healing and cleansing. For some tribes, power objects are passed down through generations. They are treated with care and respect because shamanist communities believe in the power that these objects can give to them (Mackinnon, 2018).

A trend I often see today that I consider the use of power objects (based on their use and abilities) are crystals. Stones like obsidian, rose quartz, and lapis lazuli can provide excellent energy when used correctly. Some crystals need to be recharged under a full moon, while others have to be buried in soil for a certain amount of time (McCann, n.d.). In your practice, you can definitely use crystals as power objects. Nevertheless, I would strongly recommend that you do your research and find a crystal that best supplements your intent.

Spirits

There are three types of spirits that you will encounter in the shamanic dimension: spirit guides, spirits of ancestors, and spirits of nature. They serve different purposes, but they are all integral in shamanism, even in your contemporary practice.

Spirit Guides

Most shamanic schools do not consider spirit guides as separate from animal, ancestral, and nature spirits. However, Mackinnon (2018) defines them as beings of the upper world. They are ethereal spirits who carry universal wisdom. Like I mentioned in Chapter 3, they can help you find purpose and meaning, provide guidance and insight, and grant inspiration when you seek them.

Spirits of Ancestors

Ancestral spirits are deceased ancestors who come back to the physical world to help shamanic tribes preserve memories and tradition. A shaman can seek the counsel of ancestral spirits, but it is still his or her task to apply their teachings to the community's current situation. The purpose of ancestral spirits is to provide collective wisdom so that the present generation can learn from their experiences (Mackinnon, 2018).

Spirits of Nature

The spirits of nature pertain to the essence of everything you find in nature. Again, we go back to the shaman's worldview. Remember that everything is made of energy and has a spirit. From a tree to a flower to the sky to the water, shamans can pick up the energies that come from these natural elements. It is the shaman's task to define the energy and to determine how to use it in his/her work (Mackinnon, 2018).

Calling the Spirit Forces

There are four fundamental requirements for calling the spirit forces: purpose, trust, energy, and interpretation.

Purpose

Before you begin contact with the spirits, you must first identify the purpose of the call. Do you have a question that you want to ask? Do you need healing in your mind, body, or soul? Are you looking for direction or guidance? You need to have a clear purpose when you initiate contact with the spiritual forces so that they can give you more informed advice. Be as specific as you can so that they, in turn, can give you more accurate answers. Here are a few examples:

- **Don't ask:**

"Is this the right career path for me?"

- **Ask:**

"Will this job give me fulfillment and financial security?"

- **Don't ask:**

"Should I move to a new city?"

- **Ask:**

"Which city will help me grow and evolve as a person?"

- **Don't ask:**

"Please give me energy."

- **Ask:**

"Please re-energize my body, give me mental vigor and strength, and inspire my creativity so that I can fulfill all of my tasks in the coming week."

Trust

Trust is vital in talking to the spirits. If you don't trust the spirits, how can you trust the advice that they will give you? It is impossible to build a mutually beneficial relationship with the spirits (or with anyone for that matter) if there is no trust between both parties.

However, I do understand if you have anxiety over making initial contact. Like any other new adventure, taking that first step can be a little nerve-wracking. So let me assure you: There's nothing to be afraid of. As you grow in your training, it will be easier to distinguish friendly spirits who are willing and eager to assist you. Shamanic helpers are waiting for you. Use your instinct to find them in the lower and upper worlds.

Energy

We communicate with the spirits through transferring (or sharing) energies. This process can have physical manifestations such as uncontrollable body movements, nausea, or feelings of ecstasy. But you must be willing to open yourself up and absorb the energies that come from spiritual forces. The first few times may have intense manifestations. It really varies from person to person—but you will learn how to receive these energies in a more balanced way as you progress in your training.

Also, you shouldn't force connections, especially when you're a beginner, to avoid any adverse effects. What this means is that you want to proceed lightly when you're just starting to explore the spiritual realms. As you hone your skills, you will get more comfortable in interacting with different spirits. But you should begin your shamanic journey in the most pleasant way you can, whatever that means to you.

Interpretation

Lastly, you must be able to interpret what the spirits are trying to communicate with you. They can show you images or make you feel things. Their messages can come in the form of vibrations or dreams. They can lead you to a new place, and it's your job to figure out how it applies to your situation.

As I mentioned earlier, your intentions must be clear when you initiate contact with the spirits. This will actually help interpret what the spirits want to tell you. The more specific your purpose is, the easier it will be to interpret the spirits' answers and revelations.

Creating an Altar and Clearing Your Space

When you create an altar, you're not doing it for the aesthetic. It is actually a spiritual activity, and it sets the tone for your intentions. This is the physical space where you will train to improve your shamanic abilities, where you will perform rituals and ceremonies, and where you will interact with the spirits.

Here are the steps to create your personal altar:

1. Find a quiet corner in your home that you can dedicate to your shamanic works. It doesn't have to be a big space—just enough room for you to meditate (and maybe occasionally perform ceremonial dances).

2. Clear this space of all clutter. There should be no distractions so that you can focus on your shamanic journey.

3. Get a rug, shawl, scarf, or any decorative cloth that feels sacred to you. It shouldn't have bright colors or distracting patterns so as not to take away from the calmness of the space. Lay it on the floor or hang it on the wall behind you. (You can use two fabrics if you want.) It will help in setting the tone of the space.

4. Bring your power objects into the altar. The energies they produce will empower you during your shamanic journeys. Just use your intuition to determine where you need to put each object, except for those that need sunlight or moon-

light to recharge. For these items, I recommend that you place them close to a window. If your space doesn't have a window, bring in a salt lamp (or any type of lamp with a dimmer), although you might still need to recharge these items in natural light from time to time. In the last part of this chapter, we will talk about what regular items you can use as power objects.

5.I also suggest that you bring in objects that can open up the portals to the spiritual realms. For example, incense produces smoke that can help you access the upper world, while a bowl of sand, which you can dig into, can help you access the lower world.

6.Use herbs like sage to keep your altar clean and pure. Burning sage will also drive away evil spirits from your altar.

Follow these steps to prepare your altar at home. Once you're done creating your altar, you can use it right away to train, meditate, and journey into the spiritual realms.

Daily Ritual to Connect with the Spirits

You don't always have to perform a ceremonial dance to be able to connect with the spirits. There are simple rituals that you can incorporate in your daily life to be able to cultivate your relationship with the spirits, like meditation, setting intentions and minimalism.

Meditation

The first and most effective daily ritual in connecting with the spirits is meditation. You should spend 10 to 20 minutes every day at your altar. Practice mindfulness and breathing exercises so that you can hone your shamanic abilities as well as sharpen your patience, concentration, and other related skills.

Intentions

When you wake up in the morning, take a moment to set an intention for the day. What ultimate goal do you wish to achieve? What's one task that you want to finish before the day ends? Maybe you've wanted to try new things or to visit a new place. Whatever your intention for the day is, write it down on a piece of paper. Declare it to the universe or do both. Then spend a few minutes meditating on it and seek the guidance of shamanic helpers so that you make it become a reality.

Minimalism

As I mentioned earlier, materialism and consumerism have led us away from nature. Our material possessions create cravings that distract us from the essential things in life.

As part of your shamanic training, you can slowly adopt a minimalist lifestyle so that you can get rid of these unwanted distractions and desires. Look at all you own and remove items that don't serve your purpose anymore. Simplify your lifestyle so that you only have what you need.

This doesn't mean that you need to get rid of every frivolous thing, but you do need to unlearn your current relationship with material things. They shouldn't control you. They shouldn't define who you are. You are not what you own.

In addition, you need to be more conscious of how and where you allocate your time, energy, and money. If something doesn't contribute to your growth as a practitioner of neo-shamanism and as a human being, you should disassociate yourself from it.

Embodying Energy in Matter: Power Objects

Three things define a power object:
1. Power objects are sacred (to the shaman);
2. Power objects contain energy;
3. Power objects can be examined with your senses.

In traditional shamanism, power objects are either inherited or found by the shaman in nature. These include plants, flowers, stones, sticks, and feathers.

In neo-shamanism, you can also use regular objects that fall under the definitions as mentioned earlier. For example, a crystal is a sacred stone that contains energy. You can hold it in your hand, feel its texture, and look at it with your eyes.

Other examples include candles, statues or figurines, and a family heirloom. The last one can help you connect with your ancestral spirits.

When you perform shamanic rituals, you can gather the energies that come from these power objects. Note, however, that not all power objects are suitable for all rituals. You have to determine which power objects serve the purpose of the ceremony. In some cases, if you use the wrong power object, its energy can actually prevent you from making a strong, secure connection with the spirits.

FIVE

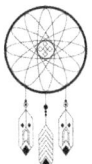

The Shamanic Journey

LET'S QUICKLY RECAP THE FOUR TYPES OF JOURNEYS THAT A shaman can take:

- A mental journey involves both thoughts and emotions. It activates the alpha waves of the brain.
- A physical journey consists of using our five senses to observe the reality. It activates the beta waves of the brain.
- A soul's journey involves entering and exploring the spiritual realms. It can be intentional or involuntary, and it activates the theta waves of the brain.
- A spiritual journey involves unlocking the higher self and achieving enlightenment. It activates the delta waves of the brain, which are usually activated during the fourth stage of the sleep cycle called deep sleep.

In this chapter, we will address how you can embark on a shamanic journey more comprehensively. The first part of this chapter speaks about how you can establish your place of power. In particular, what can you do before, during, and after the journey so that you can continuously grow as a practitioner of neo-shamanism?

Meanwhile, you can find some tips on how to connect with your spirit allies in the second part of this chapter. It is divided into two sections: the lower-world power animals and the upper-world teachers and guides. Like I mentioned before, I want you to focus on the lower and upper worlds during your training. This section will help you get more familiar with these realms and the spirits that inhabit them.

With all of that said, let's start our conversation about the shamanic journey.

Establish Your Place of Power

A shamanic journey is not like a lazy stroll at the park. To establish your place of power as a shaman, you need to be ready. Not only for the journey itself but also for what happens before and after it. In this section, I will walk you through the processes involved before, during, and after the shamanic journey.

For the purpose of our discussion, we will use the lower world as the setting, although these processes will be applicable in a voyage to the upper world as well.

Before the Journey

There are four things that you need to prepare before you embark on a shamanic journey—your mind, intention, altar, and opening.

Mind

The great irony of the shamanic journey is that you need to let go of control to be able to gain control of your shamanic abilities. Simply put, you need to have an open mind before you enter the lower world. You can't visit the spiritual realm with the mindset of a tourist. You can't force the spirits to follow a definite schedule and list of activities.

Instead, travel into the lower world with the mindset of a child. Let your curiosity and intuition guide you through the different paths, landscapes, symbols, and images that the spirits will reveal to you.

Here's another piece of advice: Try your best not to be anxious about the journey. Remember what I said about our thoughts and emotions being connected? If you have any negative feelings before you enter the spiritual realm, like anxiety or fear, you will likely attract negative thoughts during the journey. This can prevent you from establishing a clear connection with the spirit helpers. Worse, you might attract evil spirits when you enter the lower world.

So breathe, relax, and be excited about what awaits you in the spiritual realm. A positive mindset is key in establishing your place of power.

Intention

Next, set an intention for the journey. We talked about purpose in the previous chapter of this book. When setting your intention, you have to be as clear and specific as possible so that the spirits can give you the answers that you need.

Altar

We also talked about how you can create a shamanic altar in the previous chapter. Before you start your journey, make sure that everything in your altar is in the right position. If you need to light some candles so that you can use them as power objects, then do so at this point. You may bring relevant power objects closer to you so that you can absorb their energy better. You can also play shamanic drumming songs during this step. The sound will make you feel more relaxed and ready for the ceremony.

Preparing your altar before a shamanic journey is a ritual in itself. So take your time and be intentional in where you place your power objects, how you set the tone, and where you plan to sit to meditate.

Opening

Lastly, prepare your opening to the spiritual realm. Like I said in the previous chapter, you can use a bowl of sand as your entry point to the lower world. But if you don't have a physical object to use as an opening, that's fine. You can visualize the opening in your head. Think about a cave, for instance. Imagine walking into the cave. What sensations will you feel? What sounds will you hear? What will you see as you descend further into the cave?

For this technique to work, the image must be clear inside your head. If you find it hard to picture an opening using your imagination, you can do a visualization exercise before you embark on a shamanic journey. You can look at pictures and/or watch videos of people exploring caves. Better yet, visit one yourself and then use the memory of this trip whenever you want to enter the lower world.

During the Journey

Once you've opened your mind, set your intention, prepared your altar, and chosen your opening, you are ready to begin your shamanic journey. Because it is a ritual, I've found that following a specific set of steps really helps me in entering an altered state of consciousness that takes me to the lower world. Here is an overview of what I do during a ritual:

1. I set a timer for 10 to 15 minutes, and then I sit at my altar in a lotus pose with a thin cushion under me. I make sure that I am comfortable in my position, but not so much that I would fall asleep during the ceremony.

2. I close my eyes to prepare for meditation. When I do my ritual during the day, and the sun is too bright, I use a blindfold to help me stay focused.

3. I start the ritual with a few minutes of mindful breathing. I use the technique that I taught you in Chapter 3—breathe in for seven seconds, hold for four seconds, and then breathe out for another seven seconds. I also listen to the drumming song that's playing in the background. I try to match my breathing to its rhythm.

4. I think about the intention that I had set before I started the ritual. I also verbalize it several times like a chant.

5. Once my thoughts are focused on my intention, I visualize an opening to the lower world. I imagine a cave, or a well, or the roots of a tree. Whatever portal I choose for the ceremony, I make sure to take my time in traveling through it. I explore every inch and welcome the sensations that come to me.

6. After I pass the portal, I usually find myself in a natural landscape. This is how I know that I've entered the lower world.

7. I begin to explore my environment. If I am in a forest, I feel the forest floor beneath my feet. I touch the trunks of the trees and notice how rough they are against my fingertips. I listen to the sound of the wind blowing through the branches and leaves above me. I pay attention to the other sounds as well. Is there a brook nearby? Are there birds chirping? Are there animal spirits wandering in the forest with me? I open up my senses and take my time exploring the lower world before I make contact with the spirits. If there's a dark energy close by, I retrace my steps and follow a different path.

8. Most of the time, a power animal reveals itself to me voluntarily while I'm exploring the lower world. It will follow me around if it wants to make contact with me. So if I see a spirit animal several times while I scout my surroundings, I know that I can approach it. (Note that in most cases, if an animal spirit reveals itself to you repeatedly, this the power animal that you're looking for.)

9. I seek the counsel of my power animal. I ask it the question that I need the answer to. It will reveal its advice to me in many different forms, and it is my task to interpret the message. When I was a beginner, I would often be confused about what a power animal was trying to tell me. But I soon realized that an unclear purpose caused this. I was also asking questions that were too broad. Now that I know how to set a clear intention and to request a specific question, I don't need to make an effort to understand what the power

animal's message means anymore, no matter what form it takes.

10. I spend time with my power animal for as much time before the timer goes off. I seek its wisdom and listen intently to its advice.

This is the 10-step process that I follow during the journey. Note, however, that this might not be exactly how your journey will go. It is always different for everyone, so trust your instincts and do what feels right for you.

After the Journey

When the timer goes off, you will slowly return to the physical world from your journey. For this part, I personally spend another five to eight minutes of reflection on what I saw and learned in the spiritual realm. I stay in the lotus pose and go over the message that my power animal has shared with me. I try to recall specific moments from my journey that I think is significant to my intention and question. More importantly, I spend some time thanking the power animal that has helped me in my journey. I also give thanks to any other shamanic helpers that I encountered during my time in the lower world.

When I'm ready to be fully in reality once again, I like to listen to a more rapid drumming pattern. The quicker rhythm helps in transitioning your brain from your alpha or theta waves, which are relatively slower, to your beta waves. (Before you start your journey, you can create a playlist that is perfectly timed to your ritual.)

On some occasions, I will feel the need to write down any information or memory that I think is important. This helps me in remembering what I discovered just in case I encounter a similar situation in the future. Journaling your shamanic journey can also help you keep track of your progress as a practitioner of neo-shamanism. To effectively track your progress, list down how you felt, what extraordinary things you saw, what challenges you encountered, what key learning you took from the experience, and what shape your power animal has taken.

Connect with Your Spirit Allies

You know by now that building a good relationship with power animals in the lower world and spirit teachers and guides in the upper world is key to your growth. Without their guidance and support, you will never be successful in your shamanic journey.

There are several techniques that you can implement to better connect with your spirit allies. I will share with you some of the methods that have proven to be effective in my own personal training.

But before we dive into the specific techniques for the lower and upper worlds, let me share with you some of the things that I do in general:

1. The first technique I use in connecting with shamanic helpers is to meditate at a specific time of day or night. This helps in getting me into the right headspace for the shamanic journey.

2. I remove any distractions from my altar. For example, if there's a lot of outside noise, I wear headphones and play drumming or meditative songs to cancel them out. I also cover items in my home that distract me from my practice. I will put a blanket over my TV if I feel like it's disturbing my concentration. I also put my gadgets in silent mode and/or put them in another room.

3. I take a break when I need to. I did this often when I was just starting because I found that some of my journeys were a little bit mentally and emotionally draining. This does not mean that I also took a break from exercises that cultivate my shamanic abilities. I still meditated consistently, but I paced myself when it came to embarking on a shamanic journey. Like your body and mind, your soul also needs to recharge.

Power Animals of the Lower World

To have a better connection with the power animals of the

lower world, surround yourself with totems that remind you of the creatures that you have encountered in this realm. For example, if an elephant has helped you in a quest, you can get an elephant figurine. If you've encountered a leopard, a piece of leopard-print cloth can be your totem. If an eagle has been in contact with you, put together a bundle of feathers. A power animal can inhabit a totem in the physical world or transfer some of its energy to the object. This allows you to stay connected to the power animal even if you're not traveling regularly to the lower world.

You will also discover that power animals come in different forms whenever you visit this realm. An eagle might be flying the first time you encounter it, but it can spend a whole journey perched on a tree the next time you visit. In another voyage to the lower world, you might see that it's ablaze but not actually burning. These imageries have different meanings depending on what your intention is. So, as often as you can, write about your unique experiences and what your interpretations of them are.

The last thing that I do to cultivate my connection with power animals is to make a habit of thanksgiving. After every journey, I spend some time thanking them for their guidance and assistance. I recognize their generosity, kindness, and wisdom. Then I tell them that I look forward to seeing them again on my next journey.

Upper-World Teachers and Guides

Spirit teachers and guides in the upper world might be more elusive than power animals in the lower world. I have found that being more vocal about my intention while in the upper world is effective in drawing them out. When I sense good energy in the upper world, I humbly call out to it and ask it to reveal itself to me.

Once I've made a connection with a spirit helper from the upper world, I like to turn down the volume or stop the music that I'm playing. I just want to focus on the energy of the upper-world spirit. It's just me and the spirit in that ethereal place. I open myself up to its abundant wisdom and expect nothing more than what it's willing to reveal to me. Their messages are usually beyond what I've anticipated anyway.

After our conversation, I will also give thanks to the upper-world teachers and guides. I humbly excuse myself before returning to the physical realm.

SIX

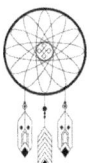

Psycho-Spiritual Work Between the Worlds

SHAMANIC WORK ISN'T ONLY SPIRITUAL—IT ALSO DEALS WITH our psychology and can even have therapeutic effects depending on how you practice it. Meditation, altered states of consciousness, and shamanic journeys are exceptional at removing negative feelings like fear or anger and replacing them with positive feelings like joy and compassion. They also trigger "healing responses and other recuperative potentials" (Winkelman, 2010) that can further assist in psychological development and growth.

Based on experience, shamanic work has provided me with a safe space to express my feelings, let go of negative emotions, and heal from traumatic experiences. The training aspect of shamanic activities has also made my mind stronger. I have discovered how to deal with stressful events in a much healthier way. My general disposition in life has also improved since I started practicing shamanism and living by its guiding principles. But I am getting ahead of myself.

In this chapter, we will discuss the different stages of transformative journeys. I will also teach you how to integrate these journeys so that you can have a holistic experience and maximize the psycho-spiritual benefits of shamanism.

Transformative Journeys

When you embark on a shamanic journey with the purpose of transformation, there are four stages that you need to go through. These include retrieving the soul, releasing negative energy, healing from pain and trauma, and developing your overall psychological well-being.

Retrieving

Soul retrieval has been part of the shaman's work since the early days of shamanism. People believed that illnesses were caused by evil spirits who steal someone's soul. It was the shaman's job to find the evil spirits that took the soul, to coax them into giving the soul back, and to bring it back to the sick person so that the healing process could begin (Harvey & Wallis, 2016). In most cases, soul retrieval is required when a person has gone through a traumatic event. Domestic abuse, near-fatal accidents, and unexpected deaths can lead to the separation or fragmentation of the soul.

If you believe that you've lost part of your soul due to trauma, then you need to start your transformative journey with soul retrieval. You should set it as your intention before you begin the ritual so that spirit helpers can clearly show you the way towards the missing part of your soul. Often, if not all of the time, a lost soul hides in the darker corners of the lower world. So you might need to convince an evil spirit to set your soul free.

If most or all of your soul have gone missing due to a particularly harrowing experience, you will need the help of another shaman to retrieve it. Remember that traveling to the spiritual realms is a soul's journey, so you can't possibly go to the lower world without most or all of your soul. It will be extremely dangerous to try to enter the spiritual realms when you're at your most vulnerable. In this case, find someone you trust and let them perform the ritual for you.

Releasing

The next stage of transformation is to release negative

emotions, thoughts, or energies that are holding you back. A traumatic experience may be associated with grief, guilt, shame, sorrow, anger, hate, misery, agony, jealousy, addiction, helplessness, resentment, etc. You have to let these feelings go —set yourself free from the anchor that's been weighing you down.

One of my favorite ceremonies to perform during this stage of the transformative journey is a fire ceremony. The flames and the smoke can take you to the upper world where enlightenment awaits. The upper world is a great place to visit when you're holding onto adverse feelings that you can't let go. This bright and pastel-colored realm will remind you of who you were before tragedy struck so that you can remember what it was like to not be carrying all of this negativity with you.

To perform a fire ceremony, you can start a fire in a safe environment. You can use a candle if you're indoors or create a fire pit outdoors if you have the space. Remember to prioritize your safety when performing a fire ceremony!

On a piece of paper, write about the traumatic experience that you recently went through. Be as detailed as you can so that you can release all negative feelings that are associated with it. When you're finished, read through what you've written. Remembering the trauma can bring it to the surface so that you can more easily let it go.

Then set the trauma ablaze. Watch the piece of paper burn into flames and smoke. During this step, call to the spirits of both the lower and upper worlds and ask them for healing. This leads us to the next stage of transformation.

Healing

Healing is one of the significant traditional roles of shamans in their community. They learned how to use and channel energies to be able to cure illnesses within their tribes. Aside from physical diseases, healing can also be provided in the areas of emotional, intellectual, social, and spiritual well-being (Warber, Bruyere, Weintrub, & Dieppe, 2015). In neo-shamanism, healing remains a necessary stage in the transformation process.

During this stage, you need to look through your shamanic toolbox and find the right skills and tools for the situation. You will likely need the assistance of power animals and shamanic helpers both from the lower and upper worlds. Some power objects can also have healing effects on the mind, body, and soul. Listen to your intuition when figuring out how to properly go through this stage.

Developing

Lastly, you reach the point of development. This is when you complete your transformation. With a desire to change your current situation and the discipline to meditate and perform other shamanic activities that contribute to your goal, you will realize one day that you have completed this stage. It may not happen overnight, but you'll see that everything has been made new because you persisted.

How to Integrate Your Journeys

If you haven't noticed already, all four transformative stages are connected to each other. They are all part of a single process. But to give you a clearer idea of how to integrate the stages of your journey, let me give you an example.

Let's say that you've recently gone through a distressing event — for example, a death in the family. You may have to travel to the lower world to retrieve a part of your soul that profoundly mourns the loss of your loved one. Release the grief that you carry in your heart before you can start healing. Including developing a new identity that doesn't primarily depend on the person you lost.

It may take some time before you can go through all four stages of a transformative journey. Some processes can take weeks, months, and even years to complete. But the great thing about shamanism is that you don't have to go through it alone. You have the guidance of your power animals in the lower world. You can find solace in the upper world and seek wisdom from the spirit teachers. And you can practice meditation in the physical realm whenever feelings of sadness overwhelm you.

This is how you integrate your journeys. You apply the techniques that you have learned from the previous chapters of this book to get through the four stages of transformation. When you have a clear map of where you are and where you want to go, the only thing that's left for you to do is to, well, go.

SEVEN

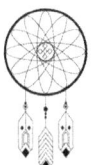

The Power and Beauty of Ceremony and Ritual

CEREMONIES AND RITUALS ARE A POWERFUL TOOL IN shamanism. They can be performed by the shaman alone or with the community. We talked about the significance of ceremonies and rituals in Chapter 3. In this chapter, we will talk about the most common traditional ceremonies and rituals, how the ceremony works its magic, and how to create your own ceremonies.

Traditional Ceremonies and Rituals

In this section of the chapter, I want to discuss three traditional ceremonies and rituals that shamans performed to help their communities: a sacred plant ceremony, a traditional sound ceremony, and a trance-dance ritual. These could be done alone or combined together, depending on the intention that was set beforehand.

Sacred Plant Ceremony

A sacred plant ceremony involves the use of plants with psychoactive properties that help the shaman in entering an altered state of consciousness. Plants like ibogaine, San Pedro cactus, peyote cactus, psilocybin mushrooms, and the ayahuasca brew can heighten the shaman's senses. Activate a dream-like state, and trigger an emotional journey that leads to self-discovery, among other effects. We will discuss these five sacred plants in more detail in Chapter 12.

In the modern era, sacred plant ceremonies are considered taboo because of the very same characteristics that proved beneficial for shamans and their communities. Governments ban or control the use of these sacred plants because of their psychoactive properties, which is understandable considering that most people don't use them to embark on shamanic journeys.

However, in a sacred plant ceremony, your intention is essential. You shouldn't be using these sacred plants if your only motivation is to get high. This often leads to a "bad trip" that induces negative physical symptoms (like nausea and vomiting), frightening hallucinations, and false visions.

To be able to establish a safe and strong connection with the spirits through a sacred plant ceremony, you have to respect the plants that you are using. So meditate and reflect on why you're performing the ceremony in the first place. Before ingesting the plant, you have to prepare not just your body but also your mind and soul. Make sure that your heart is in the right place so that you can find the correct answers to your questions.

Traditional Sound Ceremony

We discussed the significance of vibration and sounds in Chapter 4. Shamans use them to engage different wavelengths in the brain, depending on which journey they want to undertake. The most common instrument among native tribes is the drum. It is common for shamans to have a personal connection to their instruments.

Traditional sound ceremonies usually involve a drumming circle. This creates a sense of connectedness among community members that add to the sacredness of the ceremony. The drummers play a repetitive rhythmic beat that begins slowly but steadily picks up pace as the ceremony goes on. This allows the participants to enter a trance state that is a prerequisite to healing, journeying, divination, and other shamanic works. Their heartbeats will also increase in speed following the rhythm of the drumming pattern.

At the height of the experience, they can be playing three to seven beats per second. The participants reach a euphoric state. An overwhelming sense of calmness overtakes them. This is when they have the most substantial connection to the spirits.

Past the peak, the drummers will slow down the beat to allow their souls to return from their journeys. The tempo will continue to decrease until the end of the ceremony.

You don't have to learn how to play the drums for you to perform a contemporary adaptation of a traditional sound ceremony. Shamanic drumming songs and other related music are available on the internet. You can find them on YouTube, Spotify, and other video and music streaming platforms.

Trance-Dance Ritual

Like music, dancing, and movement activates different wavelengths in the brain that allow participants to enter a collective trance state. Aside from enabling an altered state of consciousness, a trance-dance ritual also has therapeutic benefits. We will discuss these benefits further in the next chapter.

There are five stages in a traditional trance-dance ritual: preparation, breathing exercise, trance in motion, motionless trance, and reintegration. We will also discuss these stages in more detail later on, but just to give you an idea, here is an overview of each stage:

1. Preparation involves preparing the body, mind, and soul for the ritual. During this stage, participants will have to set an intention for the ceremony.

2. Rapid breathing starts slowly but then picks up pace in time with the rhythmic pattern of the drums.

2. Trance in motion is when the dancing begins. In some cases, participants follow a particular choreography. In others, they just let the energy dictate their movements.

4. Motionless trance is when participants are still in a trance state, but their bodies become still. This usually happens after the peak. When the tempo of the drums begins to slow down, so will their bodies.

5. Reintegration is the process of returning back to reality. The participants wake up from the trance and reflect on the experience.

How Ceremony Works Its Magic

Scientists will reject "magic" as a possibility because observable facts can not explain it. They use brain imaging and other scientific and medical tools to quantify the effects of these ceremonies and rituals and to explain them in "real-world" terms.

However, shamanism requires us to believe in the supernatural. Not only that, it forces us to see that the supernatural is, indeed, not as "super" as science would have us believe. Reality and magic are not mutually exclusive. They cohabit the universe. In your practice, you will realize that the shamanic worldview is made up of energy. The belief that all things in the universe, even those we can't see, have a spirit. Everything and everyone interconnected, are sacred and always evolving, and are real—is actually true.

As human beings, our abilities are limited. Our bodies and immediate surroundings are like chains that hold us back from the greater truth. Our physical forms cannot travel across realms. Like I said earlier, the realms are not like a three-story house where you can just walk up and down the stairs to access each world.

The role of ceremonies and rituals is to act as a tool that allows us to tap into the magical side of the cosmos. They are the keys that open up the chains and set us free. They remove the limitations presented by reality so that we can explore realms that are beyond scientific understanding. They allow us to defy the laws of nature within the physical realm and to interact with the unseen forces that are at work in the universe.

Ceremonies and rituals in themselves are not magical. It is the intention that makes the difference. You can get high on hallucinogenic plants, play the drums, and/or dance without causing an altered state of consciousness that connects you to the spiritual realms. In other words, the magic lies in your intention. For a ceremony to work its magic, you need to have a clear, unselfish, and higher purpose.

Before we end this section, a quick note regarding the difference between ceremonies and rituals: So far, we have used the words "ceremony" and "ritual" interchangeably. However, some practitioners will argue that a ceremony is a unique event, whereas ritual is a habitual event. I personally don't mind that they are used interchangeably. However, for beginners, it might be beneficial to differentiate between the two.

Some ceremonies, like a sacred plant ceremony, are not frequent, i.e., you don't perform them regularly. You only use sacred plants for specific purposes, so you should consider their usage as a ceremony. Meanwhile, some practices need to be formed into habits, like meditation. Trance-dancing was also considered a ritual in some tribes because they performed them during specific times (like full moons, season changes, or harvest time).

How To Create Your Own Ceremonies

There is no specific formula in creating your own ceremony. It will always turn out different from the last. But there are six necessary steps that I like to follow as the foundation of my ceremonies. These include preparing for the ceremony, creating the altar, making an offering, opening the sacred space, performing the ceremony, and closing the sacred space.

Prepare for the ceremony

You already know one of the first things that you need to do to prepare for a sacred ceremony is to set an intention. Healing, celebrating an achievement, thanksgiving, manifesting an aspiration, retrieving a soul, or guiding a soul to transcendence are just some examples of the kind of intentions that people usually set before a ceremony.

During this step, you should also design the ceremony. What ritual best suits your intention? Is meditation enough to achieve your goals? Or do you need to perform a more elaborate ceremony using sacred plants, music, and/or dance?

Create the altar

In Chapter 4, we already discussed how to create an altar. You should already have it set up for the ceremony. If not (or if you're doing the ceremony outside of where you set your permanent altar), then take this time to set the sacred space where you plan to perform the ritual.

(Note: The steps in Chapter 4 included lighting sage, or a similar herb, to cleanse and purify the space before the ceremony. We will save this for later when you're ready to open the sacred space.)

Make an offering

Depending on your intention, you might want to make an offering to the spirits before you begin the ceremony. This will make them more willing to help you on your journey. If you're dealing with evil spirits (like in soul retrieval and exorcism), an offering will also appease these spirits, making it easier for you to work with them.

There are many different things that you can offer to the spirits during this step. Native tribes used to provide animals that they hunted to show humility and establish trust with the spirits. In your ceremony, you can offer fresh flowers, fruits, or vegetables. You can fetch water from a nearby lake or river. You can also light incense sticks or candles. Coffee, tobacco, honey, milk, and herbs are typical offerings as well.

The key here is to make the offering meaningful. How

does it represent your intention and/or relationship with the spirits that you are trying to communicate with?

Open the sacred space

Light a sage so that you can cleanse, purify, and open the sacred space in preparation for the beginning of the ceremony. You can also open the space by playing instruments (like a drum or a rattle), singing, humming, or chanting. Again, you can always use a playlist from the internet. Lighting a candle or incense, meditation, and mindful breathing, and interacting with your portal to the spiritual realms will also open up the sacred space.

Perform the ceremony

Now you can perform the ceremony. This is where the process always varies. You can perform each of the traditional ceremonies and rituals that we discussed earlier or a combination of them. You can also perform other forms of ceremonies and rituals if you know any.

When you make contact with the spirits, don't try to take charge of the interaction. Humbly express why you are trying to communicate with them and then let them guide you through the rest of the journey. After all, you are a visitor in the spiritual realms, and they are inhabitants of it. They know the ins and outs of their home. The best thing you can do once the connection is made is to listen, pay attention, and let them show you the way.

Closing the sacred space

Lastly, you need to close the sacred space. You can do this by thanking the spirits that have helped you, spending a few minutes of reflection, and blowing out the candles if you lit any. This is an essential step in the process, so don't skip it. The last thing you want is to leave the portal open for evil spirits to just come through it.

Ceremonies and rituals allow us to interact with the spiritual realms and its inhabitants. Therefore, we must perform them respectfully and with an open mind. The reason we use tools such as sacred plants, vibration and sounds, and dance is so that we can give up control and let the spirits guide us through the journey. Our altered states of consciousness enable us to be more susceptive to the message that the spirits are trying to reveal to us. Through ceremonies and rituals, we can honor the sanctity and importance of this interaction.

EIGHT

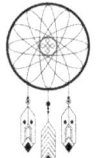

Dancing with Spirits

DANCE IS BENEFICIAL NOT MERELY FOR THE BODY BUT ALSO for the mind and soul. In fact, psychologists have recently recognized its therapeutic benefits. Dance/movement therapy (DMT), also called movement psychotherapy, has been proven to support a person's intellectual and emotional functions on top of his or her motor functions. The difference between this and regular dancing is that the former is not just a form of exercise—the choreography is meant to mimic language. Through movement, the mind uses the body to communicate both conscious and unconscious feelings. It allows a person to express what's inside his or her mind without having to say a word. It also creates a safe space to process thoughts and emotions that may have felt overwhelming or threatening if dealt with otherwise (Gleissner, 2017).

Shamanic tribes have been using dance as a form of therapy for thousands of years. They used dance in sacred ceremonies because it created a group dynamic that enabled a collective experience of an altered state of consciousness. The psychosocial aspect of dance also encouraged community engagement among members of the tribes. Aside from these, dance even:

- Relieving frustration, tension, and stress
- Released repressed desires and energies
- Lead to emotional catharsis and abreaction
- Generated feelings of revitalization and tranquility
- Encouraged expressive liberation and creativity (Winkelman, 2010).

In this chapter, we will discuss dance as a ceremonial and ritual tool that not only the shaman but the rest of his or her community used.

Traditional Trance Dance

As I mentioned earlier, dance is a vital component in a lot of shamanic ceremonies. It allows participants to collectively enter a trance state and, in some cases, to end the trance as well. Spiritual journeys can also be acted out in dance, like the soul retrieval ceremony of the Paiute tribes in Northern America. Aside from spiritual journeys, dance was also used for ceremonies for healing, divination, exorcism, and worship. The dance was often combined with music, chanting, and other ritual activities (Bourguignon, 2004).

To give you a more unobstructed view of what a traditional trance-dance ceremony entails, let's look at specific examples from tribes around the world.

West Africa

The Fon tribe in Niger, the Dogon tribe in Mali, and the Shilak tribe in Nigeria performed traditional dance ceremonies for several reasons, including worshipping their gods, finding witches to prevent crimes, controlling dangerous forces of nature, and uniting themselves with cosmic forces (Papadimitropoulos, 2009).

South Africa

In Botswana and Namibia, the Sans people performed healing trance-dances for individuals and the community as a whole. Their traditional routine involved a group of healers dancing in a single file while the women of the tribe sat around a bonfire and sang rhythmic medicine songs. The healers would sometimes attach rattles to their legs to further enhance the vibrations that they need for the ceremony. As they entered an altered state of consciousness, they would feel the pain they're trying to heal and would, as a result, scream in agony. However, the pain would be replaced by a healing energy as they continued the trance-dance. They would then channel the healing energy by touching those with sickness or who needed healing. As the healers transferred the healing energy, they would absorb the illness and then shout, releasing the illness into the air. Aside from diseases, this trance-dance ritual was also used to settle disputes and other internal problems in the tribes (Evans, 2019).

Inuit

The Inuit used shallow, one-sided drums to accompany their ceremonial dances. These drums were made with the skin of a caribou. Sometimes it came from the lining of the stomach or bladder of a walrus. It was then stretched over a wooden hoop. To perform the ceremony, a group of up to 60 people would gather inside giant igloos. The shamans would lead the participants in song and dance that were meant to connect them with the spirits of nature. Sometimes, two women would perform throat singing, which was done by producing sounds from their throats and chests. They would sing in different registers and create a rhythmic pattern that served the ritual ("The Inuit," n.d.).

Korea

In Korea, the goal of their traditional trance-dance was two-fold. First, the shamans used dance to communicate with the spirits. They made "whirling movements" to the left to connect the physical realm to the spiritual realm. They let the energy flow from their chests to their fingertips. By repeating this movement, the shaman was able to enter shinmyon, which is what Koreans called the trance state. This signified that he or she had made contact with the spirit. From the "whirling movements," the shaman would move his or her arms upwards while an almost painful emotion appeared on his or her face ("Shamanistic Dance, Purposeful Ecstacy," n.d.).

Taíno

The Taíno tribe in the Caribbean performed a traditional trance-dance ceremony called areítos to communicate with their ancestors. The ritual was led by a priest/healer whom they called a behíque. They used a mayohuacan, a wooden drum, to create rhythmic beats and drank sacred brews, both of which helped them in entering an altered state of consciousness. The primary purpose of the ritual was to mediate the relationship between the living and the dead. Through dance, participants were able to exchange energies with their ancestors so that they could live harmoniously (Morejón, 2018).

As you can see, these native tribes have different methods of performing a trance-dance ritual. However, as you will see in the next section, there are notable similarities in these rituals and others that guide us in our contemporary adaptations of these traditional ceremonies.

Contemporary Adaptations: Dance Yourself Awake and Free

Before we talk about the modern adaptations of traditional dance rituals, I want to quickly discuss some of the reasons why you should perform this ceremony. As I see it, there are three significant reasons why you need to connect with the spirits through dance:

- Physical. Dance is a form of exercise that can help you improve your endurance. You can also relieve the physical symptoms of stress and anxiety through dance.
- Mental. Sometimes, our minds can get in the way of us experiencing the spiritual realms as we

should. Dancing helps you to get out of your brain for a while. While your brain (the muscle) focuses on the movements, your mind (the consciousness) can go on a journey without restrictions.
- Psychosocial. Dance creates a sense of community that makes the ceremony more sacred and allows the participants to enter an altered state of consciousness collectively.

So how exactly does trance-dancing translate to our neo-shamanic practice? As I said earlier, there are five stages to a traditional trance-dance. Contemporary adaptations still follow this structure, so let's discuss each step and how to do them properly.

Preparation

Some practitioners like to fast beforehand so they can avoid nausea and vomiting during the ritual (especially if they are using sacred plants along with the dance), while others do stretches and other physical exercises. During this stage, you should also set an intention so that you have a clear purpose for the ritual.

Rapid Breathing

To safely perform rapid breathing, you start slowly at first. Play a drum song that's intended for a dance ritual. You should time your breath to the beat of the drums, which start at a slow tempo. Then, as the rhythm picks up speed, you match it until your breathing and heartbeat are at the same pace.

If you don't have an accompanying drum or song, you can still perform rapid breathing by counting your breaths. In the beginning, you can perform the mindful breathing exercise that we discussed earlier. Follow the seven-four-seven count, then slowly increase the speed until you reach a one-two-three-four-three-two-one tempo. You should be able to inhale and exhale within this cycle, no holds in between.

You can also apply this technique with an accompanying song.

As you perform rapid breathing, let the energy vibrate throughout your body. You will begin to feel the movement reverberating from your core. When you reach this point, it's time for you to enter the trance in motion.

Trance in Motion

As the name suggests, trance in motion involves movement. You begin to sway, turn, wave—whatever movement feels right for you. Let the beat dictate your rhythm as your energy connects with the spirits'. You don't have to have a specific choreography, although it wouldn't hurt if you have something prepared.

However, don't be too concerned about the steps of the dance. The most important thing during this stage is to channel your energy into the intention that you had set before the ceremony began. If the energy calls for you to shout, then shout. If it calls for you to sing, then sing. Let your intuition and/or the shamanic helpers guide you during this stage.

At the peak of this stage, you will reach a euphoric state.

Motionless Trance

After you've reached the peak, your heartbeat and breathing will start to slow down. The drumming song, if you played any, will have slowed down at this point too. You're still inside the trance and connected to the spirits, but euphoria will make you feel relaxed and at ease. You may even sway side to side if that feels right for you. You may lie down, sit in lotus pose, or rest in child's pose. Again, let the energy and/or shamanic helpers show you what to do. You don't need to think it through.

Reintegration

Reintegration involves coming back to reality after the trance. The time it takes for you to transition from the motionless trance to reintegration will vary in every ceremony. Don't try to control it because this ceremony is all about letting go of control. Until the very last stage, just let the spirits guide you through the journey. When they've shown you everything they want to reveal to you, they will tell you when it's time to go.

As you reintegrate, thank the spirits for helping you achieve your goals. Allocate a few minutes of reflection and think about the experience. What did you learn? Did the ceremony meet your expectations? If not, what do you think needs to be improved? For example, I have learned that at the beginning of my training, my thoughts prevent me from fully immersing myself in the ritual. If this is your problem too, you need to keep practicing meditation.

Dancing with the spirits is a sacred ceremony that allows us to perform important shamanic works. When we use a trance-dance ritual to, say, heal others, we are not actually the ones who are curing their sickness. Remember, we are simply channels of energy. With dance, the spirits funnel their healing powers through us. So consider this experience a privilege. It's an honor to be able to help other people on behalf of the spirits.

NINE

The Medicine Wheel

THE MEDICINE WHEEL IS A SACRED OBJECT THAT IS COMMONLY used for health and healing. But it also serves different functions in a shaman's ceremonial work. It represents the four directions, the interconnectedness of all beings in the universe, harmony and balance, etc. The significance of the medicine wheel depends on which tribe it belongs to, but we will discuss its most common usage and interpretations in this chapter. Overall, it is a symbol of hope.

Before we discuss its specific interpretations, let's talk about what a medicine wheel looks like. In most tribes, the medicine wheel is made of stones. It has three main components: a cairn in the middle of the wheel, an outer ring that marks the perimeter of the wheel, and two perpendicular lines that divide the wheel into four quarters ("Medicine Wheel," 2018). Some communities may change or add elements to this basic structure, depending on their cultures. But these three components are always present in most medicine wheels.

The Circle and the Diagonals

The circle is a sacred shape in a lot of ancient civilizations and indigenous societies. You can see it in drum circles, healing circles, stone circles (megalith formations), and crop circles. In shamanism, the outer ring of the medicine wheel can refer to many things, but, in most interpretations, it represents the Earth and its boundaries. It can also represent the cycle of life, which we will discuss in-depth in Chapter 11.

Meanwhile, the diagonals represent the Sun's path. They divide the medicine wheel into four directions, which bear a lot of significance in the interpretation of the medicine wheel itself. You will also notice that the diagonals intersect at the center of the circle. The intersection represents the center of the Earth or the axis mundi.

The Powers of Four Directions

The medicine wheel is divided into four quarters by two perpendicular lines. The lines point to the four directions, which are North, West, east, and South. The four directions have varying meanings among and within tribes. Here's an example of what the four directions of the medicine wheel can mean to a specific tribe (Dapice, 2006):

Direction/
Interpretation
East
South
West
North
Human Aspect
Mental
Emotional
Physical
Spiritual
Color
Yellow
Red
Black
White
Animal

Eagle
Red-tailed Hawk
Bear
White Buffalo
Medicine
Tobacco
Cedar
Sage
Sweetgrass

ASIDE FROM THESE INTERPRETATIONS, the four directions of the medicine wheel can also pertain to the stages of life (birth, youth, adulthood, death), seasons (spring, summer, winter, fall), and natural elements (fire, air, water, earth).

To interpret what the medicine wheel wants to reveal, a shaman will walk around it repeatedly and use it as a map to integrate the different aspects represented by each quarter and how they all connect to one another. Shamans will perform ceremonies specifically for the interpretation of the medicine wheel. During the ceremony, they will ask shamanic helpers to help them recognize the path that the medicine wheel is trying to direct them to.

Each journey begins in the East, where the Sun rises. This represents the beginning, spring, and birth. Because this is the direction where the Sun rises from, it is associated with light and the upper world. This direction is where wisdom and insight can be gained.

The shaman then travels counter-clockwise to the South. When the Sun is at its zenith, this is the direction that receives the most light. It represents growth and summer birth to a child, a seed to a tree, a bud to a blooming flower. The South is where curiosity and creativity can be found.

Now the shaman heads to the West, the darkest quarter of the medicine wheel. It is where the Sun sets, and the shadows lie. It represents the fall and stands for transition. When there is an internal conflict that needs to be sorted out, this is where the shaman works.

Lastly, the shaman travels to the North, the direction of night and winter. Because the wintertime is the time of hibernation, this direction stands for reflection. The shaman looks back at the year that has been and recognizes how one season has led to another. This is also where the shaman works to ask the spirits for joy, abundance, and sustenance for the year ahead.

The shaman can spend time in a single direction if that's where the work is needed. A shaman will set up an altar in the East, for instance, if he or she needs some wisdom and guidance from the upper-world spirits.

The Human Aspects of the Wheel

Now let's look at each direction as they pertain to the human aspects. Looking back to the table, you can see that the East relates to our mental aspect, the South pertains to our emotional aspect, the West pertains to our physical aspect, and the North pertains to our spiritual character.

East - Mental

The East represents the mental aspect of the human condition. As I mentioned earlier, this is where the shaman seeks wisdom and insight from the upper-world spirits. The shaman works here when education is devalued, and there is a loss of experiential learning. To address these problems, the tribe can promote supportive education and provide an accurate history of their community. The shaman can seek the help of ancestors to help with the latter solution.

South - Emotional

The South direction represents the emotional aspect of the human condition. This is where growth, creativity, and curiosity can be found. The shaman works here when there is a loss of identity within the community. He or she will also deal with stress, anxiety, depression, and other related disorders in this direction. A dance ritual can be performed in this direction in order to drive away the evil spirits that bring about these disorders to members of the community. The shaman may also offer counseling to those who are suffering from emotional distress.

West - Physical

The West direction represents the physical aspect of the human condition. If you remember from the earlier section, this is the direction that catches most of the shadow. Quite literally, our bodies are what cast shadows when we face the Sun, which is probably why this direction is associated with the physical aspect. Anyway, this is where the shaman works when there is a weakness, physical illnesses, and other related problems in the community. To address these problems, the shaman may use herbal medicine to treat sickness. He or she will also seek the help of the lower world spirits to administer the proper method of healing.

North - Spiritual

Lastly, the North direction represents the spiritual aspect of the human condition. This is where the shaman works when there is a loss of faith and hope among community members. These problems may arise from traumatic experiences such as famine, natural disasters, and war. To help his or her community, the shaman may perform a sacred plant ceremony to re-center their religion again.

To apply these learnings to your neo-shamanic training, you can use a simple wooden hoop to represent the circle and two strands of string to represent the perpendicular lines that create the four directions. You can also draw the medicine wheel on a piece of paper. In one of your meditative rituals, bring the medicine wheel into your altar and use it as a map for your journey. Take along your spirit helper around the circle. For each human aspect that the four directions represent, what areas do you need to improve? What areas need healing? What areas have been abundant recently? Ask your spirit helper for guidance when you want to find solutions for problem areas and thank them for when you have been experiencing success in one or more of these human aspects.

Additionally, the power animal that helps you in each human aspect may change as you walk around the circle. Refer to the table when you're looking for the right spirit animal for each direction. In the East, you want to search for an eagle. In the South, you want to search for a red-tailed hawk. In the West, you want to search for a bear. And in the North, you want to search for a white buffalo.

Of course, these animal forms may still change when you travel around the medicine wheel during your journey. Always keep your eyes open for what spirit animal reveals itself to you.

TEN

Spirit, Soul, and the Sacred in Nature

WE'VE ESTABLISHED THE IMPORTANCE OF NATURE IN shamanism. Believers of this religion respect nature a great deal and treat it as they would another human being. After all, everything in nature has a life. This is one of the guiding principles of shamanism.

In this chapter, we will talk about the sanctity of nature. How do our spirit and soul connect to nature and its elements? Is there a way to connect with nature even if we live in an urban setting? These are just some of the questions we will be answering in our discussion of the spirit, soul, and the sacred in nature.

An Earth-Based Traditional Cosmology

How the universe became to be is one of the biggest mysteries of life. No one really knows the answer to this existential question because no one was there to witness it. But cosmology offers several possibilities.

Cosmology is the examination of the origin and evolution of the universe. It looks into the different theories regarding the creation of all beings, including scientific and theological approaches to creation. In the early days of cosmology, humans believed that the Earth was the center of the universe. (We discussed the axis mundi in Chapter 3, which reflects this ideology. Before science proved that the Sun is, in fact, the center of the galaxy, indigenous peoples and ancient civilizations marked their own calculations of where the axis mundi is.) It was Nicolaus Copernicus who first challenged the geocentric model. In the 16th century, he proposed the heliocentric model (named the Copernican Model after him), which implied that the Earth and the other planets in the galaxy revolve around the Sun. Meanwhile, in theology, monotheist religions believe that a Supreme God created the universe and everything in it. Most of them believe in ex nihilo creation, which you will learn more about in the next chapter (Halvorson & Kragh, 2017; Redd, 2017).

In shamanism, cosmology is much more complicated. As you will see in Chapter 11, there are different models to shamanic creation stories. Different tribes believed in different gods, demigods, and spirits. Some of them believed that these supernatural beings created the universe out of nothing. Some of them thought that life started from a cosmic egg. Some believed in world parents—two gods that came together to give birth to existence. Others found that life emerged from the Earth or the waters (Leeming, 2010).

The common ground among shamanic tribes around the world is the belief in the existence of the three worlds—the upper, middle, and lower worlds. With these came the idea in cosmic trees, power animals, power objects, shamanic helpers, godlike spirits, etc. All of these concepts are integral to the shaman's cosmology.

The main difference between the shaman's cosmology and the other approaches to cosmology is that the former is more Earth-based. Let me explain: The Big Bang Theory states that the universe began as a single point of hot particles, light, and energy that expanded over time. The Earth was just a byproduct of this expansion (NASA, 2019). Meanwhile, the

Christian Bible states that God didn't create the Earth until the third day of creation.

In most shamanic creation stories, the Earth was the starting point for all creations; hence, the geocentric model of the universe was propagated.

Even though science has proven that the Earth is not the center of the universe, we still consider in the geocentric model of the universe as neo-shamans. Why? Well, first let me say that we know that the Earth is not the center of the universe. We don't reject scientific data and proof. However, we treat Earth as if it is the center. This belief makes Earth more critical. It establishes the sanctity of the Earth, nature, and its inhabitants. It helps us to remember that we should respect the planet we live in.

So when I say that the cosmology of shamanism is Earth-based, I don't mean that we have to ignore what science tells us. I mean that we have to believe that the center of life is the Earth. Our existence and survival depend on our relationship with nature.

The Starving of Our Sacred Earth Souls

The sacred Earth soul pertains to the collective consciousness, energy, and soul of our planet that all living things, which includes human beings, are connected to. It's a concept that is consistent with the shaman's worldview. Like a baby in the mother's womb, we are connected to Mother Earth via an umbilical cord that sustains us. Our very existence depends on this relationship. Without it, we can't survive.

However, modernity has created a gap between the Earth and us. We are not as connected to nature as we used to be. We talked about this problem in Chapter 2 when we discussed the shaman's worldview.

Ages ago, native tribes would only get what they needed from nature. They never took more than what they needed to sustain their community. When their environment was low in resources, they would find another place to settle in to give their old home time to recover and to flourish again. In return, they had thanksgiving ceremonies to honor the gifts that nature had given them. They also gave back to nature; they took care of their environment and nourished it as it would do for them.

Today, consumerism and materialism precede nature. Every year, 6.5 million tons of trash enter the oceans (World Ocean Network, n.d.). Illegal mining and logging are leaving our forests barren. The Amazon, which is where 20% of the planet's oxygen comes from, is literally on fire. Farmers are burning the forests for more pasture land. In the past year, there has been a 278% increase in deforestation in Brazil alone, and the government is not doing anything about it (Sullivan, 2019).

Technology has made the gap between Mother Earth even bigger and us. People are more dependent on their gadgets than they are in nature. Every day, most of us wake up and fall asleep with a black mirror in hand. We fill our homes with more gadgets that allow us to stay in for as long as we want.

We can buy anything through our phones, too—clothes, groceries, and food are all just a tap away. Because of this, we don't have to go out and be in nature anymore. This makes us way less concerned about how materials are sourced. We don't consider sustainability as a priority when we make a purchase. It's all about convenience: "How soon will this product arrive at my door?" It doesn't matter if natural resources in third-world countries get depleted, if waste materials pollute their environment, or if their children have to work instead of going to school. If you can get it by tomorrow, that's all that really matters.

Our sacred Earth souls are starving. Mother Earth is crying for help. As a species, we have abandoned our relationship with nature. I think it's time to go back.

If we don't do anything to restore our relationship with

nature, we will continue to starve our sacred Earth souls. If this keeps happening, we put our very existence at risk.

Contemporary Shamanic Nature Work and Tools

From the previous section, two fundamental questions arise: What can we do to restore our relationship with Mother Earth? How do we stop our sacred Earth souls from starving?

Because most of us don't live close to nature anymore, we have different social and spiritual training than traditional shamans. This doesn't mean that there's nothing we can do to solve our current problems. Contemporary shamanism recognizes the power of ancient practices but reframes them into a more relevant context that applies to the modern age. To be able to reclaim our relationship with nature, we don't need to abandon our current possessions. We don't need to leave our cities when resources are low.

As I see it, there are four contemporary shamanic nature works and tools that can help us nourish our sacred Earth souls.

Retreat

As often as you can, go on a nature retreat so that you can reconnect with Mother Earth. This is a great way to meditate on your relationship and to nourish your sacred Earth soul. We'll discuss this more in the next section.

Conservation

Conservation pertains to the protection of sacred lands and natural resources. This work has been particularly challenging in recent years because governments prioritize oil pipelines and other commercial uses of land over its sanctity. In Canada, an oil pipeline expansion over Trans Mountain in Alberta was approved by Prime Minister Justin Trudeau. The project will cover 715 miles across sacred lands (BBC News, 2019). Meanwhile, Mauna Kea in Hawaii is threatened by the Thirty Meter Telescope project that would desecrate the tallest mountain on the island (Lam, 2019).

As neo-shamans, we need to ask ourselves, "What can I do to help conserve nature?" Here are a few actionable steps:

- Donate to organizations that aim to protect nature and its resources.
- Be outspoken about the desecration of sacred lands that are currently happening around the world. Use modern tools, like social media, to bring awareness to these issues.
- If this type of desecration is happening near you, you can join a protest or start a petition to stop it.
- Minimize the waste that you contribute to the environment. You can do this by using a tote bag when shopping, bringing reusable water bottles and straws wherever you go, only buying perishable food items that you're going to consume, and other similar actions.
- If possible, use cruelty-free and/or organic products. These products have a less negative impact on the environment.

Sustainability

Sustainability pertains to providing the needs of the present generation without putting future generations at risk. This is an essential task for us as practitioners of neo-shamanism. We are not here on this planet for just a lifetime; our souls will return to the cosmos, and our descendants will remain connected to us as we are with our ancestors. Therefore, it is our responsibility to prioritize sustainability in the here and now.

There are several ways that we can live more sustainable lives. Here are a few ideas:

- Stop supporting fast fashion brands. They have negative environmental impacts like water

pollution, toxic chemicals, and textile waste. In fact, textile dyeing is the second-largest source of water pollution around the world (Perry, 2018).
- On the topic of fashion, buy second-hand clothes at the thrift store as much as you can. Don't buy brand new clothes unless you absolutely have to.
- If you need to buy new clothes for a special event, purchase them from sustainable brands like Aritzia, Alternative Apparel, and Pact.
- Reduce your energy consumption by turning off lights and appliances when you're not using them.
- Subscribe to paperless billing for credit cards, utilities, and other bills.
- Cook food seasonally so you can support local farmers. They often have more sustainable ways of farming than mega-farms.
- Walk, bike, use public transportation, or carpool rather than driving alone or hiring an Uber everywhere.
- Stop ordering things online. The packaging alone produces so much waste. The delivery also adds to the carbon footprint of the product. Is your convenience worth the damage that online shopping causes to the environment?
- Reuse, reduce, and recycle as much as you can.

Thanksgiving

Thanksgiving is an important ceremony in most, if not all, native tribes. You can perform a traditional thanksgiving ceremony, or you can find other ways to thank the environment. Here are a few ideas:

- Plant a tree. You can make this an annual tradition.

- Grow a garden. This will help bees and other insects in nature. You can also grow your own food.
- Start a compost pit. You can nurture the soil around you.
- Volunteer at a community garden, for a cleanup drive, or a restoration project.

These are just some of the ways that you can bring traditional shamanic principles into the modern age. If you can find other ways to nurture your sacred Earth soul and to protect Mother Earth, try to incorporate them in your life too.

Reconnect with the Sacred Nature in Nature and Your Own Nature

Whether you're in nature or far from it, you can still reconnect with the sacred nature and deepen your spiritual relationship with Mother Earth. In this section, we will discuss three steps that you can take in order to nurture that relationship: retreat, meditate, and sit and observe.

1. Retreat in nature.

The first thing you can do is to go on a nature retreat. Go camping. Spend a weekend at a mountain lodge. If you live close to a beach, make a habit of visiting even if only for a day. Spending time in nature is one of the most effective ways to recharge your sacred Earth soul. By surrounding yourself with Mother Earth's energy, you can reconnect with her life force.

2. Meditate in nature.

While you're on a nature retreat, allot some time to meditate. Remove your shoes to feel the grass or sand beneath your feet. Find a quiet spot to sit so you can ground yourself in nature and then breathe the air around you. Listen to the sound of the waves crashing against the shore or the rustling of leaves above you. The wind is whispering something in your ear. Do you hear it? While you meditate, let Mother Earth embrace you with her life-giving energy.

You can also meditate in nature even if you're not physically in nature. When you meditate at home, you can visit the lower world, which, if you remember from our earlier discussions, often appears as a natural landscape. It will also help if you have a playlist of natural sounds to listen to while you meditate at home.

3. Sit and observe nature.

Sometimes, all it takes for us to reconnect with nature is to sit and observe how magnificent it really is. Look at all the life around you! The trees you see are most likely older than you—imagine the history they've witnessed! Look at the sky, the clouds that float, and the birds that fly above your head—how free they must feel to just be in nature! Look at the sea, the lake, the river—they all sustain a whole other world underwater! You are surrounded by life. It breathes, it moves, and it feels. Do you see it?

ELEVEN

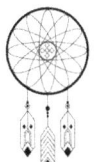

Embedded in the Cycle of Life

Some religions have a clear definition of the afterlife, like Christians and Muslims who have a concept of heaven and hell. Others believe in reincarnation, like Buddhists and Hindus, who believe in Karma and how it determines what an entity's next life is going to be.

In shamanism, life doesn't end in death—there is no afterlife in heaven or hell. At the same time, life doesn't take another form after death—people are not reincarnated based on their previous good or evil deeds.

Instead, shamanism believes that death is embedded in the cycle of life. It is not the end of life but merely a stage in it. Our essence comes from the universe, and we will go back to it when we die. Like the Law of Conservation of Energy, shamanism believes that energy can neither be created nor destroyed. Since we are all made of energy, it will just be transformed into some other form that continues to exist in the universe.

In this chapter, we will talk about what all of this means. Specifically, we will discuss where life came from according to shamanism, how we remain connected to our ancestors who came before the descendants and us who will come after us, and what death truly means in shamanism.

Creation Stories: The Power Formation Myths

Christianity says that God created the whole universe in six days and rested on the seventh. Meanwhile, Islam has two theories regarding the beginning of life: creationist and evolutionist. The former is akin to Christian belief wherein Allah created the whole universe in six days and rested on the seventh, while the latter believes that the "days" actually refer to long periods, giving room for evolution as Charles Darwin described it (Catchpoole, 2002). In Greek mythology, Gaea (the Earth
) was born from the void and gave birth to Uranus (the sky) who populated the world with her. Ancient Egyptians, Mesopotamians, and Norsemen have their own versions of how all creation started with a body of water. The Chinese believed in the story of P'an Ku, who hatched from a cosmic egg; he kept growing for 18,000 years, and he got so tall that he broke and fell into pieces. His body parts created the Earth ("Creation Stories," n.d.).

Although shamanism is a widespread religion among indigenous tribes around the world, it is highly nuanced when it comes to the mythology of creation. Unlike most religions, it doesn't have a single creation story. Tribes have different cultures and, therefore, have different myths about where life came from.

For instance, the South Pacific New Hebrides believed that the creator of life sang a song to separate heaven and Earth. According to Netsilik Inuits, a considerable flood drowned all life on Earth. This is similar to the story of Noah and his ark in the Bible. All that remained were two shamans who repopulated the planet after one of them shape-shifted into a woman.

Siberian Tungus tribes believed that there was only water before there was anything else, and then God sent down a fire that burned part of the ocean, thus creating land. (Leeming, 2010).

Though creation myths are widely different, there are five recurring themes among shamanic tribes (Leeming, 2o10):

- The "ex nihilo" creation story states that life existed out of nothing.
- The "chaos" creation story says that there was chaos before there was life, and life existed from primal elements or a primal object.
- The "world parents" creation story states that parents birthed the world after their union, separation, division, or sacrifice.
- The "emergence" creation story says that life came out of a hole in the Earth.
- The "water-divider" creation story states that the gods created life out of primordial waters.

In some cases, it is possible that two or more of these themes were present, like in the creation story of Netsilik Inuits, which had elements of the "water-divider" and "world parents" creation stories. And although they are not as cohesive as the creation stories of more "structured" religions like Christianity and Islam, these mythologies served as the foundation of the identities of indigenous peoples around the world. They explained how existence came to be, which made life less mysterious than it would have been and shaped the way of life of native tribes.

If you haven't noticed, you can also find these themes in creation stories from other ancient civilizations, like the Greeks, Egyptians, Mesopotamians, Norsemen, and Chinese. Even the story of creation in the Christian Bible, Jewish Tanakh, and Muslim Qur'an were ex nihilo.

Expand Your Sense of Self: Find Your Own Creation Myth

Creation stories shaped the culture and the way of life of native tribes. In your neo-shamanic training, you should sit down and write your own creation myth to expand your sense of self. This exercise will help you to get to know yourself better and to discover parts of your identity that you may not have known existed. It forces you to look back at your most pivotal memories and experiences and how they shaped the person you are today.

For me, there are five distinctive elements in writing your own creation myth:

- Point of view
- Beginning
- Challenges
- Magic and symbols
- Past, present, and future.

Point of view

You should write your creation myth in the third person. Treat yourself as an omnipresent narrator so that you can write the story more objectively and prevent your current thoughts and feelings from influencing the narrative.

Beginning

You don't have to go as far back as your birth (world parents, union) to write the beginning of your creation story, although you can do this too if you want to. But I would suggest that you look back at the turning point in your life when you realized that you needed to make a change. Was there a feeling of emptiness (ex nihilo) or turmoil (chaos)? Were you at the lowest point of your life (emergence)? Were there patterns in your family that you didn't want to follow (world parents, separation/division)? Was there someone who helped you get out of your current situation (water-divider)?

Challenges

What challenges did you have to overcome since that

turning point? How did you overcome them? Are there any challenges that you haven't conquered yet?

Looking back at these challenges can be emotional, but you must not let it stop you from writing your own creation myth. Instead, take this as an opportunity to celebrate the strides you have made towards self-improvement. You can also recognize the people and spirits who have helped you make it this far.

Magic and Symbols

Even if we currently live in a world of scientific discoveries and technological advancements, magic and symbols still play a significant role in our practice of neo-shamanism. You may not have noticed them before, but they have always been there. Always working alongside you during the high and low moments of your life.

You will have to answer a lot of questions when writing your own creation story, but none of them is as important as the existence of magic in your life. Look back at your lowest of lows. Was there ever a moment when you didn't know how you would get out of a difficult situation? Still, somehow, you managed to overcome it. You can call that luck. Christians will say that it's grace. But whatever it was, it was magic—you were able to do what you thought back then was impossible.

You also have to remember that you are not writing an autobiography. You are writing your own creation myth. So use symbols to tell your story and translate the magic in your life into your writing.

Past, Present, Future

Lastly, you have to look at yourself as a fish swimming downstream in a river. It moves from the past to the present to the future. These identities are all connected. Even though the fish has left upstream, is currently swimming midstream, and wants to reach downstream, it is still swimming in the same river. The fish and even the water may change, but life is continuous, always flowing.

So ask yourself: How did your past experiences shape your present identity? And how do you plan on evolving in the present to achieve your ideal future self?

Widen Your Circle: Connect with Ancestors and Descendants

In shamanism, the ancestral world is still very much a part of the community. Because death is not considered the end of life, native tribes believed that their ancestors naturally transitioned from one reality to another. As I've mentioned before, shamanism believes that energy is not created nor destroyed. This is why the family members who came before you, despite the fact their physical bodies have already passed, still exist in the cosmos. Their essence is transformed into energy that you can tap into to gain wisdom. When your physical body passes, your descendants will also be able to connect with you.

There are several ways that you can connect with your ancestors and descendants. Let's start at the most inherent connection of all—your DNA. You've been literally carrying your ancestors with you since birth, and your descendants will carry you with them when they are born. By studying your genealogy, you gain insight into your family's origins and history.

Through your lineage, some traditions and heirlooms have been passed down from generation to generation. For example, let's say that your grandmother's grandmother started a tradition of throwing a family gathering every holiday season. Wherever everyone is, you all come home for a week to celebrate together. Even if you, your parents, or your children never got the chance to share this tradition with the person who started it, you're all still connected through this shared memory. I've also mentioned in Chapter 4 that you can use family heirlooms as power objects that you can use in shamanic ceremonies and rituals. It possesses shared memories too. It serves as a bridge between the physical and ancestral worlds.

You can also connect with a specific ancestor by building a shrine for them. When performing a ceremony, you can put a totem in your altar that represents that ancestor so that you can find and communicate with them in your shamanic journey. You can use a photo, a piece of clothing, or any item that they considered special. Part of their essence will forever remain in that item. In the same way, if you want your descendants to be able to connect with you, you can choose an item that you want to represent you and pass it on to the next generation.

Death as a Part of Life: The Gifts We Receive When Facing Death

In shamanism, there is no such thing as death, at least not in the sense that most people perceive it. Shamanism believes that death is simply a process of transition. Our bodies go back to the Earth, but our soul is immortal. It remains part of the cosmos.

As practitioners of neo-shamanism, this belief gives us comfort. It removes our fear of the "impending doom" and allows us to experience and appreciate life in the present. If sickness plagues us, we can look forward to not feeling physical pain anymore. We will be free from the suffering that our bodies feel. We will be free to continue our cosmic journeys as souls.

We also make an effort to nurture not just our bodies and minds but also our souls. Remember that you also have a responsibility to be present for when your descendants need you. You'll be able to witness the continuity of your lineage because your soul remains forever.

Some shamans will also say that death allows us to reach enlightenment. Without the limitations our physical bodies present to us, we can take on a spiritual journey and seek our higher selves more freely.

Working with Death in Shamanism

As a neo-shaman, your primary role is to guide the souls

of those who are on the verge of death. To show them that death is not the end of life but merely a part of it. You can perform a ceremony to show the soul which way to go so that they can transcend peacefully into the ancestral world. If the person is a family member, you can seek the help of your ancestors to reassure the individual that he or she is not leaving the world behind. Instead, he/she is coming home—family is also waiting on the other side.

You also play a role in comforting those who will be left behind. You will help them in processing their grief. You can do this by building a grief altar. If your family has a property, choose a little section of land where you can all gather for a ceremony. Place a totem in that place, like a huge lidded vase that can contain all of your grief. Remove the lid and then ask your family members one by one to express their sadness, anger, or any other negative emotion that they currently feel because of the death of your loved one. When everyone has had their turn, close the lid and end the ceremony in prayer.

Pray for the person you lost. Pray that they find their way. Pray that they are at peace so that they can transcend into the ancestral world and not the lower world. Pray that everyone in your family can find comfort in knowing that you are all still connected to that person, even if they aren't with you anymore. Pray for healing. Pray for strength. Pray for peace. Following this leave the totem behind.

Alternatively, you can use a bonfire to let all the negative emotions float like smoke into the air. After everyone has spoken, light the bonfire and play the drums to drive away from the heaviness in your hearts.

TWELVE

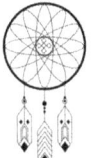

Sacred Medicinal Plants

SHAMANISM PRE-DATED SCIENCE AND MEDICINE AS WE KNOW IT today, so shamans depended on medicinal plants for cures and healing. They also used plants, specifically those that have psychoactive properties, to achieve an altered state of consciousness for rituals and ceremonies.

In this chapter, we will discuss traditional plant ceremonies, what sacred plants both traditional and contemporary shamans use, and how to safely use these plants in your practice.

Traditional Plant Ceremonies

Traditional plant ceremonies are sacred activities that shamans undertake with a specific purpose in mind. Sacred plants are not intended to be used for recreational purposes, and shamans don't use them simply to get high. Remember that in every shamanic ceremony or ritual, the intent is very important. The plant used is just a tool that helps the shaman achieve his or her goals.

In the next section of this chapter, we will talk about how you can use five sacred plants in a ceremony with details regarding ideal settings, dosages, and possible side effects. For now, let me show you an overview of a traditional plant ceremony.

A traditional plant ceremony has four stages: preparation, ingestion, journey, and reflection/recuperation.

1.The shaman prepares for the ceremony. This step will vary depending on several factors, including the purpose of the ceremony (initiation, healing, soul retrieval, etc.) and the specific plant the shaman will be using. The shaman may have to fast, meditate, or isolate themselves from the rest of their community before the ritual begins. During this step, they will also set an intention and choose the ideal setting for the ceremony.

2.The shaman ingests the sacred plant. Different plants have different levels of potency and methods of ingestion (more on this in the next section). Some are taken transdermally or sublingually while others are eaten or smoked. Therefore, this step will vary depending on which plant the shaman uses.

3.The shaman enters a trance state and begins his journey. The journey can last for several hours, depending on the potency and half-life of the sacred plant.

4.After the ceremony, the shaman may need some time to recuperate. This step also requires the shaman to reflect. This is when he will interpret the visions, symbols, and other images that he saw during the trip.

The Sacred Plants

There are five sacred plants that both traditional and contemporary shamans use in ceremonies. They are ibogaine, San Pedro, peyote, psilocybin mushrooms, and ayahuasca. This section discusses the effects that these plants have on the human psyche and how you can use them as part of a ceremony.

Ibogaine

Ibogaine is an alkaline derived from the roots of an African rainforest shrub from the Apocynaceae family called

Tabernanthe iboga. This naturally occurring substance has psychoactive properties that indigenous people use for religious rituals. It has the potential to bring out one's instinctual side, including animal visions and sexual themes. When used in psychotherapy, it can help patients look at traumatic experiences with a more objective perspective. (Mash et al., 1998; Naranjo, 1974).

Aside from its psychoactive properties, ibogaine is also known for its ability to reverse addiction to heroin and cocaine. The first known use of ibogaine in reversing drug dependency is Howard Lotsoff in the 1960s, although his treatment was accidental. He had read about the plant and its psychedelic effects and planned to use it for another kind of trip. So he got ibogaine through a mail-order catalog. But instead of intensifying his addiction, he found that he no longer had any desire to use cocaine (Pinchbeck, 2002).

Ibogaine takes you on a very personal journey. The experience is not at all favorable, so you might want to take it alone. If you're anxious about the effects, you can have a trusted séance partner, keep an eye on you. Either way, get ready to explore memories that you might have forgotten about and to visit past experiences that may have caused present issues and trauma. Your journey with ibogaine may be a deeply emotional one, so prepare yourself for that.

There are many precautionary steps that you have to observe when you plan to use ibogaine in a ceremony. First of all, you must abstain from all types of substances at least 24 hours before the ceremony. Ibogaine can have a dangerous and even lethal reaction if you use it with other substances. These include, but are not confined to, drugs, alcohol, and caffeine. If you're using SSRI antidepressants, you will need to clean your system for at least two months before the ceremony to avoid major complications.

You should also consider having the ceremony at night because bright lights and loud noises can cause nausea during the trance. Just to be prepared, especially if it's your first time using ibogaine, keep a bucket or trash can close by.

In connection, I advise that you fast for at least eight hours before the ceremony to avoid vomiting. You should also limit your water intake beginning at the four-hour mark so that your body can better absorb the alkaloids. Make the fast a part of the ceremony, too. Use it as an opportunity to reflect and assess how your body feels, where it hurts, and what it needs.

Before you take ibogaine, clear your space of any distractions. I suggest that you perform the ceremony in bed, lying down so that you can be as comfortable as possible. Meditate on your intention and ask the spirits for guidance. Though this is more of a personal journey, it wouldn't hurt to ask shamanic helpers for assistance.

The recommended dosage for ibogaine is 15 to 20 mg per kilogram of body weight. After taking it, keep yourself open to whatever emotion dominates your mind, body, and soul. The emotion may change throughout the journey. Still, I found that ibogaine is a natural guide in itself, i.e., the journey you'll take is very intuitive, almost as if the plant becomes an extension of your intuition. Even with your eyes closed, the images you'll see will be extremely vivid. Don't get distracted by the moving objects and heightened colors. Keep your focus on your intention so you can find your way through them.

The length of the journey varies by person, but you need to take it easy for the next 36 hours or so. Don't move too suddenly, so you don't feel nauseous. To have ample time to prepare, perform the ritual correctly, and recuperate, you should allocate at least two and a half days for the whole ceremony.

San Pedro

The San Pedro cactus (scientific name Echinopsis pachanoi) is a sacred plant that is native to Peru and Ecuador. Indigenous tribes in South America have been cultivating it for more than 3,000 years because of its hallucinogenic properties. As early as 750 A.D., the Cupisniques, Chavins, Moches, Lambayeques, and other indigenous tribes in the Andes Mountains have been using it for healing, religious divination, and other magical-religious purposes (Ostalaza, Cáceres, & Roque, 2017; Pedrosa et al., 2018). Aside from its traditional uses, San Pedro is now cultivated by some farmers as an ornamental plant that contractors use for landscaping.

If you have access to San Pedro, you can prepare it yourself. Here's how:

1. Find a full-grown San Pedro plant to get two arms from. They should be about one and a half feet each. Before you harvest the arms, though, you should thank the plant for providing you the resource. Then use a knife to collect the arms. Never take more than what you need.

2. Using a smaller knife, remove the spines of the cactus, then peel off the thin translucent layer of skin around it.

2. If you look at the cross-section where you cut the arm, you will notice that a layer of dark green pulp surrounds the lighter green flesh of the cactus. Use a knife to separate the pulp from the flesh. The pulp is what you need to prepare the sacred San Pedro brew.

4. Fill a large pot with about three liters of water and place it over medium heat. Add the cactus pulp. You're going to boil it until about a cup of liquid remains, which will take about four hours. You should keep an eye on your brew to make sure you don't over boil it.

5. You will notice that the water has turned green. Filter it twice using a coffee filter to remove any contaminants from the liquid, then transfer it into a heat-proof glass jar.

6. Place the pulp back in the pot and repeat the last two steps twice more, except you're just going to use two liters of water instead of three, and you're only going to boil the brew for two hours.

7. Strain and transfer these new batches of brew into the

same jar. By this point, you should have about 300 to 500 mL of liquid.

The whole brewing process can take about seven to eight hours. Like fasting for ibogaine, you can include this as part of the ceremony and use the time for reflection. While waiting for the brew to finish, you can set an intention and write down some goals that you want to achieve during the journey.

I suggest that you perform the ceremony in the morning after the brewing process. Wake up early, before sunrise if possible, so that you can absorb the new burst of energy coming from the rising sun. Perform about 10 to 15 minutes of mindful breathing and meditate on the intention and goals that you have set the day prior.

You can eat a light breakfast before you begin the ceremony. Then drink about a quarter of the brew after breakfast. Drink the rest of the brew, a quarter at a time by the hour, until all of it is done.

It may take until the middle of the day, about an hour or two after you've drunk the last quarter before you feel the effects of the brew. It begins with slight nausea and a tingling sensation in your stomach, but you should focus more on the energy that starts to build inside you.

The San Pedro experience is mostly positive—I associate it with joy. I feel light while in it. I also feel more connected to nature and more grounded to its comforting energy. This is why I recommend that you perform the ceremony in a natural setting. A quiet campsite is ideal. A secluded beach or a private garden can also work.

This journey is primarily about seeking truths and finding clarity. It's about letting go of negative thoughts, emotions, and energies. It's about connecting with nature, its spirits, and its elements. It can be a lower or upper world journey—sometimes it is both. Follow your shamanic helpers and pay attention to what wisdom they are going to reveal. If you have a question, San Pedro will help you in translating the answer from these friendly spirits. The experience will last for about 16 hours after your last dosage, although you might peak five hours after finishing the brew.

Peyote

The Peyote cactus (scientific name Lophophora williamsii) is a sacred plant that is native in Mesoamerica. Indigenous people utilized its hallucinogenic properties for healing rituals and religious ceremonies. The Europeans' earliest record of the peyote cactus being used for these purposes dates back to the 16th century. Today, it is used as a decorative plant for landscaping. It is also harvested commercially to be processed into ointments that are mostly sold in Mexico. Because of its commercial use, peyote was declared a vulnerable species by the International Union for Conservation of Nature and Natural Resources (Schultes, Hofmann, & Ratsch, 2001; Terry, 2017).

Keep in mind peyote's vulnerable status when you use it—do not harvest more than what you need for the ceremony, and don't forget to thank the plant for providing you with resources.

You can use 20 to 30 grams of dried buttons or 100 to 150 grams of fresh buttons of peyote for a ceremony. (If it's your first time, you may use half of those amounts.) I should warn you that the cactus has an unappealing flavor. While some like to chew the buttons directly, others grind them up and then add them to juice to mask its taste. It's up to you to determine which way feels more comfortable.

I highly suggest that you find a séance partner for the ceremony even if it's not your first time. This sacred plant leads to some uncomfortable physical symptoms, like nausea and vomiting, especially during the first two hours after ingestion. Like with ibogaine, I recommend fasting before the ceremony. You should abstain from eating for at least four hours prior and use this time for reflection and meditation. Prepare a bucket just in case and try not to move too much before you peak.

The peyote plant will take you on an emotional journey that will connect you to the four elements of nature: Fire, Water, Wind, and Earth. If you encounter any of these elements during a sacred peyote ceremony, here is what each of them means:

- Fire symbolizes purification and rebirth. It will help you get rid of thoughts and feelings that create a negative self-image. However, Fire can also be a mischievous trickster who will taunt and follow you around to distract you from the journey. If this is the side of Fire that you meet during the sacred Peyote ceremony, do not run away from it. Instead, respectfully ask it to give you space so that you can focus on your intention. Finding a body of water in the spiritual realm may also help you in getting rid of the trickster.
- Speaking of water, this element symbolizes healing and nourishment. It will make you feel re-energized after the ceremony. So if you've been feeling drained and stressed, call out to Water and set rejuvenation as your intention.
- Wind symbolizes enlightenment and is usually associated with the spirits of the upper world. It will help you gain wisdom when you're feeling lost and unsure about certain life decisions. If you're currently at a crossroads in real life, you should seek Wind and ask it to blow you in the right direction during the ceremony.
- Earth symbolizes life and growth and is usually associated with the spirits of the lower world. It will help you reconnect with your core if you've been feeling disconnected from yourself. You can

seek Earth during the ceremony and ask it to reintroduce you to who you truly are.

Peyote is similar to San Pedro when it comes to the setting. It is more effective when you're in nature. So choose a natural landscape that's quiet and not busy. Let the energies in your surroundings empower you throughout the journey.

Mushrooms

Evidence of usage of psilocybin mushrooms by Mesoamerican cultures in Guatemala, Ecuador, and Mexico dates back to as early as 1000 B.C., but the Spanish, who brought Catholicism into this region, banned their usage during the colonial period (Bunch, 2009). This explains why psilocybin mushrooms, which used to be a normal part of indigenous rituals, are now stigmatized in most modern societies.

Despite the stigma surrounding psilocybin mushrooms, a lot of contemporary practitioners of shamanism still use them to achieve altered states of consciousness. It is one of the easiest to use because it is widely available and there is not a lot of preparation involved. After harvest, you can ingest the plant right away. However, a word of caution: There are poisonous mushroom species that look a lot like psilocybin mushrooms. To avoid difficulties, make sure that you are using the following species for a shamanic ceremony:

- Psilocybe azurescens is a wood-loving psilocybin mushroom that is usually found in sandy coasts. It is the most potent type of psilocybin mushrooms but it doesn't cause a lot of physical discomfort (Nicholas & Ogame, 2006).
- Psilocybe cubensis is the most frequently used type of psilocybin mushroom because of its broad availability and is easy to develop. It grows normally in warm and humid places, which is why

you'll find it in a lot of pan-tropical countries in Mesoamerica and Southeast Asia. Even though it is one of the largest psilocybin mushrooms, it is moderately potent (Nicholas & Ogame, 2006).
- Psilocybe cyanescens looks a lot like Psilocybe azurescens except it has an undulating cap margin. Like its twin, it also loves growing on wood and you will normally find it in cool and humid places. This psilocybin mushroom is moderately potent (Nicholas & Ogame, 2006).
- Psilocybe semilanceata grows in cool grassland areas. It is also called the Liberty Cap and it is one of the more potent types of psilocybin mushrooms (McGee, 2019).

Psilocybin mushrooms are also called "magic mushrooms" because of their psychoactive properties. In ceremonies, they aid a shaman in entering a dream-like state that some will describe as being similar to lucid dreaming. Mushrooms may also lead to peaceful, euphoric states that allow the shaman to see vivid visions and, in some cases, to achieve spiritual awakening.

I would suggest using half a gram of mushrooms at most in one ceremony, no matter which type of psilocybin you take. Expect lightheadedness, slight nausea, and muscle weakness during the ceremony. It might also cause paranoia and confusion to some, with the possibility of seeing frightening hallucinations. To avoid this, make sure that you have a clear intention before you ingest the sacred plant so your spirit helpers can guide you in the right direction. You might also light a sage stick to drive away evil spirits that may show you false visions.

You can perform a sacred psilocybin mushroom ceremony anywhere. If you perform it at home, make sure that your altar is prepared and that you have all relevant power objects nearby. It doesn't matter if you're sitting up or lying down, but you want to be as comfortable as you can. You should also have the ceremony at nighttime to avoid outside distractions like bright lights and loud noises. I suggest that you have the ceremony during a full moon. When combined with magic mushrooms, the energy of the full moon will help you in achieving spiritual awakening.

The effects of psilocybin mushrooms can last between six to eight hours. You should try to take down notes during the ceremony because there's a chance that you might forget some of the visions you'll see after the effects have worn off. If you're anxious about possibly seeing false and negative visions, have a séance partner keep an eye on you. They can chant, hum, sing, or use a drum to help you stay calm and focused during the ceremony.

Ayahuasca

Derived from the vine of Banisteriopsis caapi and the leaves of Psychotria viridis or Diplopterys cabrerana, ayahuasca is a type of brew or tea that is used in sacred rituals and intimate ceremonies. Indigenous tribes in the Amazon Basin use it in their spiritual journeys so they can restore lost souls and heal illnesses. Shamans in Brazil and Peru, among others, have been brewing ayahuasca since pre-Columbian times, and the tea is still being used by practitioners of neo-shamanism until today (Luna, 2003; Third Wave, Co., n.d.a).

The use, possession, and distribution of ayahuasca is illegal in the United States with the exception of religious practices if you're a member of the União de Vegetal or Santo Diame churches. It is also illegal or controlled in most countries with the exception of Brazil and Peru. In some countries, it is legal to own the plants ayahuasca is made from, but it is not legal to make the brew (Third Wave, Co., n.d.b). Because of these legal restrictions, I suggest that you go on a retreat to either Brazil or Peru so that you can legally and safely participate in a sacred ayahuasca ceremony. Although you may have to travel far for the retreat, the experience can be particularly enlightening.

To use ayahuasca, you should drink 0.5 mg per kilogram of body weight. You may increase that dosage to up to 0.75 mg per kilogram of body weight, but I would suggest that you start with the lower dosage if it's your first time. If you attend an ayahuasca retreat in Brazil or Peru, this dosage may still change depending on the advice of the shaman who will lead the ceremony.

Ayahuasca tends to drastically improve the senses while it is in effect. You will begin noticing changes within the first 30 to 60 minutes after ingestion. Your hearing and sight will be improved, which is great for communication with the spirits because you will be able to see visions and hear messages more clearly. Your skin may also tingle and you may feel energy vibrating from your fingertips.

Aside from heightened senses, ayahuasca can open your mind and make you more perceptive about your thoughts, memories, experiences, and emotions. I know people who were able to heal from trauma after a sacred ayahuasca ceremony. A friend of mine, for example, was able to remember details of a traumatic experience that his brain had blocked out for years. These details were gruesome and upsetting, but remembering them allowed him to let go and move on.

Although this type of emotional experience does not happen to everyone, you should brace yourself for it. Prepare to feel contradictory emotions at the same time, to explore memories from when you were younger, to face your worst fears, etc. This is actually one of the reasons why I suggest that you do it during a proper retreat. The guidance of an expert shaman will ensure your safety, both physically and emotionally, throughout the experience.

As you reach the peak, you will feel more and more euphoric until you reach a point of peace and clarity. At this point, your self-image may shift because of the revelations that you have received. You may also feel more connected to everyone around you. There's a possibility of sharing each other's emotions, so don't panic if you feel things that you think are not relevant to your own experience.

The effects of ayahuasca normally last for about four hours, although you might peak at around the second hour. As it leaves your system, you will be more reflective of the images you have seen.

A Word of Caution and Engagement

I have said this several times before but it bears repeating: In every sacred plant ceremony, your intention is very important. It can change the way your mind, body, and soul reacts to the psychoactive properties of these sacred plants. Therefore, you need to make sure that you're using them for the right reasons. Don't perform the ceremony if your heart isn't in the right place, or you may have a "bad trip" with a lot of physical symptoms, frightening hallucinations, and false visions.

You should also be cautious about using these sacred plants if you have a pre-existing medical condition. These plants may react with medications and other substances, which will make them unsafe to use. If addiction runs in your family or if you have a history of addiction, you should avoid using them as much as possible or seek the guidance of a trained shaman before you do. Do not ingest more than the recommended dosage to avoid dangerous and/or lethal side effects.

If you're preparing the sacred plants yourself, make sure that you do it right. Follow the steps I have provided in the previous section or do your own research regarding the best way to prepare these sacred plants. Be extra cautious when using psilocybin mushrooms and confirm that they are safe to ingest and not poisonous.

I think this goes without saying, but you should definitely check the legality of these plants in your locality to avoid any problems with the authorities. Despite the great benefits of a sacred plant ceremony, you should not break the law and risk possible jail time.

Moreover, remember that the effects of sacred plants will vary from person to person. Your intention and experience, as well as the dosage and potency of the plant, are just some of the factors that affect the experience. The effects I mentioned in the previous section are based on personal experience and the accounts of people I know.

Having said all of these, the most important advice I can give is to stay safe and be smart when performing a sacred plant ceremony.

THIRTEEN

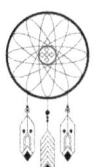

Shamanic Work in the Dream World

WE'VE ESTABLISHED IN EARLY CHAPTERS OF THIS BOOK THAT shamanism believes in the existence of realms beyond the physical. We talked about the spiritual worlds—the lower, middle, and upper worlds—and what their significance is to the shaman's work. But there is another world that shamans journey into, although often involuntarily, and that is the dream world.

The dream world is the bridge that connects the physical and spiritual realms. The shaman's journey into the dream world is mostly spiritual, given that it uses the same brain waves as sleep. As I mentioned in Chapter 3 of this book, a spiritual journey activates the delta waves of the brain. These are the same brain waves that are activated during the deep sleep stage of the sleep cycle.

Dreams and the interpretation of dreams are necessary for the shaman's work. They provide insight and answers that can't be found on a voluntary journey to the spiritual realms. In fact, in some shamanic rituals and ceremonies, trances can become sleeplike states of consciousness. Some cultures even required the shaman to fall asleep before performing a specific ritual. This is because sleep helps to make the non-physical worlds appear more vivid to the human senses (Sumegi, 2008). In my experience, I have proven this to be true. There are parts of the mind that can only be unlocked when I fully let go of control, allowing me to see things that I might not have seen before.

Two types of dreams are relevant in shamanism: normal and lucid dreams. We will talk about their significance and how the shaman uses them in his or her work in this chapter.

Normal Dreaming and Sharing

Normal dreams usually happen during the rapid eye movement (REM) stage of the sleep cycle. They produce vivid images that can seem real until you open your eyes and wake up. Normal dreams can also happen during the deep sleep stage of the sleep cycle, but these are harder to remember when you wake up because the delta waves that dominate the brain are much slower (Rosen, 2009).

Several things can happen during normal dreaming, like a false awakening, which is waking up from a dream inside another dream. Repressed desires, fears, urges, and anxieties can also manifest in normal dreams (Rosen, 2009; Turner, n.d.).

Normal dreams are when premonitions and other similar visions appear to the shaman. Spirits sometimes use our dreams to communicate with us, especially when there is an urgent matter that they need us to know. A shaman's calling can also appear in a dream. The reason behind this is that the candidate hasn't started formal training yet. Therefore they won't have the abilities needed to travel to the spiritual realms to communicate with the spirits. So the spirits reveal themselves to the candidate through his or her dream.

At the same time, two or more people can share a dream while sleeping. Dream sharing is a phenomenon that happens when two or more people either mesh their dreams or meet in a dream.

Dream Meshing

Dream meshing happens when two or more people have different dreams that have very similar details. A shared waking experience usually causes these dreams. For example, watching an episode of Survivor before sleeping can lead you and the person you watched it with to have a shared dream of living on a remote island. If this is the case, then there may not be a spiritual significance to the dream.

However, if there is no shared waking experience that can cause people to have meshed dreams, then you need to examine the dream more closely. Let's say that you and a friend both dreamed about a car accident. Use your shamanic abilities to determine whether this dream is a premonition or not.

Dream Meeting

Dream meeting happens when two people use their telepathic abilities to meet and communicate inside a dream. Shamans used this method of dream-sharing to settle arguments with each other (Sumegi, 2008). In this case, the dream is intentional. The shaman has an out-of-body experience while asleep. This skill is acquirable, and we will talk about it in the next section of this chapter.

Intentional and Lucid Dreams

When you're asleep and dreaming, but your mind is conscious that your body is in a sleeping state, that is called lucid dreaming. Simply put, lucid dreams happen when an individual is aware that they are dreaming. Some people have a lucid dream unintentionally, but there are ways to enter one on purpose. We will discuss how to have an intentional lucid dream later on in this section.

For now, let's talk about why people would want to have lucid dreams. How does lucid dreaming help you in shamanic work? Here are five reasons:

1.Lucid dreaming expands the brain. Quite literally, lucid dreaming is brain work because you're training your consciousness to wake up from sleep without rousing your body too. It takes a lot of training before a person can separate the mind and body so that she can enter the dream world as freely as she wants to. At the beginning of your training, the most difficult challenge will be to use your brainpower when your brain is working the least. The brain almost completely shuts down when you go to sleep, except for keeping your internal organs functioning while you're unconscious.

2.Lucid dreaming expands the mind. Not only will it strengthen the muscle inside your skull, but it will also unlock the incredible power of your mind. While your external faculties are at rest, your internal faculties will be at their most active. This is why people in lucid dreams can have out-of-body experiences. They leave their bodies behind and explore the world using only their minds.

3.Lucid dreaming is an altered state of consciousness. You are conscious, but you are not at the same time. It is the most complex form of an altered state of consciousness. It can really be beneficial for shamanic work, especially if you want to explore new parts of the spiritual realms that you haven't visited before. You can also stay in the dream world, which looks a lot like the physical world and meet another shaman at a specific location. This is called dream meeting, and as I mentioned earlier, shamans used this technique to settle differences and disputes. If you have a partner for this activity, you can both explore the dream world and discover new things together.

4.Lucid dreaming bridges different realities. It is the middle ground between the physical and spiritual realms. Lucid dreaming allows you to travel into these different realities more freely. It can also unlock the unconscious mind, which can change your whole perception of reality. Here, you can discover repressed or forgotten memories, which you can use in your shamanic work.

5.Lucid dreaming improves creative expression. Have you ever had a dream where you find yourself in a familiar place but it looks slightly different? Even though the dream world looks a lot like the physical world, you can manipulate it and add other elements to it when you're in a lucid dream. You can make decisions and control how the dream unfolds.

So how does one enter a lucid dream intentionally? There are a few steps you can follow. Here are some techniques that I have found most useful:

Dream Journal

When we dream, we often forget about it the moment we wake up, unless something truly remarkable happens in the dream. This is an automatic response from the brain. It helps us separate the dream world from the physical world. However, the consequence is that we find it hard to enter the dream world intentionally.

So to help you retain that connection to the dream world, you should make a habit of writing down your dreams. Start a dream journal. This allows you to remember details that you can use the next time you lucid dream. For example, your dreams might have similarities—like the same characters or places—which can help you map out the dream world. This exercise also trains your brain to keep the dream world part of your conscious mind.

Reality Check

Before you enter the dream world, you should have a reality check technique prepared. For example, you can carry a book with you every time you enter the dream world. In the dream world, one page of a book will have a different text every time you open it. In the physical world, the same page in a book will have the same text. This technique will help you differentiate between the dream world and the physical world so that 1) you don't get stuck in the dream world and 2) you know when you've finally entered the dream world.

Mnemonic Induction to Lucid Dreaming

Now let's talk about how you can enter a lucid dream. My favorite technique is the Mnemonic Induction to Lucid

Dreaming (MILD), which involves saying a phrase over and over again until you feel asleep. The phrase I use is this: "I am asleep and dreaming." By saying this phrase, your mind will remain alert and awake while your body falls asleep.

Sleep Paralysis

Inducing sleep paralysis is also an effective technique to enter a lucid dream. To do this, you need to set an alarm for the next day, placing it close to your bed. You want to be able to reach it as soon as it goes off.

Next, you should fall asleep as you normally would at night. When your alarm goes off, shut it off immediately. If you can, keep your eyes closed while you do. (This is why you need to keep the alarm as close to you as possible.) While your body is still in a sleep mode, lie in bed, keep your mind awake, and wait for your body to fall back to sleep. As soon as it drifts back to slumber, you will have entered sleep paralysis.

When you enter the dream world, you are free to explore as much as you want. However, don't cause any chaos inside the dream world and leave it pretty much as it is. This is to prevent evil spirits from finding you inside the dream. Remember that this world is a bridge between the physical and spiritual realms, so evil spirits can find you if you cause any commotion.

Conclusion

At its core, shamanism is the belief that everything in the universe is alive and interconnected—we are one with the cosmos and all of its inhabitants.

Although most people will reject shamanism as a legitimate religion in this current age of scientific and technological advancements, I hope that you have realized that it is still necessary in the modern world. In fact, we need it now more than ever. We need to reconnect with our roots. We need to reconnect with nature. We need to find the sanctity in nature again so that we can preserve it for the sake of future generations.

Before we end our conversation about shamanism, let's quickly recap everything you have learned from this book.

Traditionally, a shaman is called to serve when they possess one or more of six notable traits. If a person is born in a family of shamans, has a remarkable body feature, exhibits uncommon actions, has strange experiences, survives a near-fatal disease, and/or receives a message from the spirits through dreams or daytime reveries, he/she is called. Once a shaman receives the calling, he/she undergoes training that involves communicating with inner teachers, learning about

Conclusion

the community's myths and culture, and embarking on vision quests.

The shaman's worldview can be summarized in two doctrines: Hylozoism believes that all objects have a life, while animism believes that all objects have a mind or a soul. This worldview allows us, as practitioners of neo-shamanism, to communicate with nature and spirits. It also inspires us to treat everything in this world with respect.

To be able to communicate with the spirits, we enter the three shamanic worlds through the axis mundi, which takes the form of a cosmic tree in most cultures. The lower world is where we can find power animals who will help us in our shamanic work. Among others, they can help us see the future, predict the weather, help lost souls, and heal those with sickness. It is also where we journey for self-discovery. Meanwhile, the middle world is where the physical and spiritual worlds co-exist. Souls of the deceased who are yet to transcend because of traumatic deaths are trapped in the middle world. Therefore, you must proceed with caution when journeying into this world. As much as possible, avoid visiting the spiritual side of the middle world unless you have to. Lastly, the upper world is where the gods and demigods reside. It's the most philosophical of the three shamanic worlds, and you go here to gain insight and wisdom.

There are four types of shamanic journey that you can take: mental, physical, soul, and spiritual. These journeys have different purposes and activate different brain waves. A mental journey requires us to connect with our thoughts and emotions, and it enables the alpha waves in our brains. The physical journey requires us to use our senses, and it activates the beta waves in our brains. The soul's journey is what we embark on when we perform ceremonies and rituals, and it activates the theta waves of the brain. The last shamanic journey that we can undertake is a spiritual journey. It is

Conclusion

where we can reach enlightenment, and it activates the delta waves in our brains.

To bring the shamanic dimension into our daily lives, we can use fundamental skills and tools that traditional shamans used as well. These include ceremony and ritual, vibrations and sound, movement and dance, nature, shamanic helpers, power animals, power objects, and spirits, including spirit guides, ancestral spirits, and spirits of nature. To call upon the spirits, we must have a clear purpose, have trust in them, share our energies with them, and interpret their messages. You can also create an altar and perform daily rituals such as meditation, intentions, and minimalism to be able to connect with the spirits.

When you're ready to embark on a shamanic journey, there are things that you have to do before, during, and after the ceremony. Before the ceremony, you need to open your mind and let go of control, set a clear intention, prepare your altar, and find an opening into the spiritual world. The journey itself will be different from person to person, but I gave you an outline of the 10-step process that I follow in Chapter 5. You can follow this at the beginning of your training and slowly make it your own. After the journey, don't forget to thank the spirits for helping you. You should also reflect on what you have learned and what teachings the shamanic helpers have shared with you. It will also benefit your training if you keep a journal of your journeys so that you can keep track of your progress.

Then we talked about the psycho-spiritual work that you can perform between the worlds. There are four stages to a transformative journey: retrieving the soul, releasing negative emotions, thoughts, or energies, healing, and developing. These stages must be integrated into your journey for you to reap the benefits of your psycho-spiritual work.

To be able to do your shamanic work properly, you will have to perform ceremonies and rituals. We discussed three

Conclusion

traditional ceremonies and rituals that shamans perform: a sacred plant ceremony, a traditional sound ceremony, and a trance-dance ritual. You can perform these by themselves or combine them together, depending on your intention. While native communities have their own versions of how they perform these three ceremonies and rituals, you can create your own version by using the traditional framework as a foundation. This involves preparing for the ceremony, creating an altar, making an offering, opening the sacred space, performing the ceremony, and closing the sacred space.

In the next chapter, we took a closer look at dance. We talked about its therapeutic benefits, how native tribes performed dance rituals, and how you can perform a contemporary adaptation of a traditional dance ritual. There are five stages to a traditional trance-dance: preparation, rapid breathing, trance in motion, motionless trance, and reintegration.

We also discussed the medicine wheel and its significance to native tribes. The medicine wheel is a circular shape with diagonal lines that intersect at the center. It is usually made of stones. The four directions are represented in the medicine wheel, and they have different interpretations depending on the native tribe's culture. A common interpretation of the four directions involves the human aspects. The East direction pertains to our mental aspect, the South direction relates to our emotional aspect, the West direction pertains to our physical aspect, and the North direction pertains to our spiritual aspect. Shamans and neo-shamans use the medicine wheel as a map to identify problem areas that need healing.

Then we talked about the sanctity of nature. We can see in the cosmology of shamanism that nature was treated as sacred by native tribes. However, with modernization, people have forgotten the relationship that we have with Mother Earth and how we are connected to her through our sacred Earth souls. So I outlined some steps on how we can reconnect with nature. Through conservation, sustainability efforts,

Conclusion

and thanksgiving, we can save our relationship with Mother Earth. We can also reconnect with nature through retreats and meditation and by merely observing the magnificence of life around us.

Speaking of life, we talked about the cycle of life and how shamanism doesn't treat death as the end of it. Instead, we treat death as merely a stage in the cycle of life. When our physical bodies die, our essence will continue to exist in the cosmos. This belief gives us the foundation for working with death in shamanism. It also shows us that we are connected to our ancestors and, after our physical bodies have died, will remain connected to our descendants.

We also discussed the creation myths of different tribes around the world and how each story revolves around five themes: ex nihilo, chaos, world parents, emergence, and water-divider. At the same time, I have encouraged you to write your own creation story to help you expand your sense of self. You can do this by using a third-person point of view, beginning at the turning point in your life, going back to the challenges that you faced, using magic and symbols in your story, and connecting your past, present, and future experiences.

Sacred plants are a normal part of ceremonies in shamanic communities, so we talked about five of the most common plants that are used in these ceremonies. These include ibogaine, San Pedro cactus, peyote cactus, psilocybin mushrooms, and ayahuasca brew. You learned how to perform a sacred plant ceremony using these five plants safely and respectfully. It bears repeating: You only use sacred plants when you have a clear and unselfish intention. In shamanism, the greater good is always important, so remember to ask yourself, "How will this ceremony help me help others?"

Lastly, we talked about the dream world and how shamans used it in their work. There are two types of dreams: normal and lucid. The latter is where real shamanic work is done. We

Conclusion

enter it by writing in a dream journal, performing reality checks, using the MILD technique, and inducing sleep paralysis. Once we've entered a lucid dream, we can meet another practitioner in the dream world or explore it to find new discoveries.

All of your learning from this book will be useful in your training as a neo-shaman. However, remember that it can take months or even years before you can fully develop your abilities and be comfortable in using them. Don't be frustrated if this is the case. All things that are worth it take time.

I highly suggest that you take your time and improve your skills slowly but steadily so that you can see real progress. Focus on meditation, for example, and improve your mind's ability before you dive into more complex ceremonies like a dance ritual or a sacred plant ceremony. Use the tools that are closest to you. You don't have to completely change your lifestyle or travel far to start adopting shamanism in your life. The spirits are everywhere, just waiting for you to interact with them.

When I started writing this book, my ultimate goal was to show my readers that there is another way of living your life. You don't have to be a slave to the modern world and its frivolities. You don't need to keep chasing material things to be fulfilled in this life. You don't need to keep searching for purpose and meaning.

All you really need is nature. Come back to it, and you will see what I mean. Provisions, healing, meaning, self-discovery, and purpose—look for them in nature. Look for them in the universe. By adopting shamanism, you will find all of these things and so much more.

References

Axis Mundi. (2016). Retrieved September 3, 2019 from the New World Encyclopedia: https://www.newworldencyclopedia.org/entry/Axis_Mundi

BBC News. (2019). *Trans Mountain: Canada Approves $5.5bn Oil Pipeline Project*. Retrieved September 18, 2019 from https://www.bbc.com/news/world-us-canada-48641293

Bourguignon, E. (2004). Trance Dance. In Walter, M. & Fridman, E. (Eds.), *Shamanism: An Encyclopedia of World Beliefs, Practices, and Culture, Volume 1* (pp. 161-167). Santa Barbara, CA: ABC-CLIO.

Bremmer, J. (2016). Shamanism in Classical Scholarship: Where Are We Now?. In Jackson, P. (Ed.), *Horizons of Shamanism: A Triangular Approach to the History and Anthropology of Ecstatic Techniques* (pp. 52-78). Stockholm, Uppland: Stockholm University Press.

Bunch, K. (2009). *Psilocybin and Spiritual Experience* (Clinical dissertation). Alliant International University, San Francisco, CA.

Catchpoole, D. (2002). The Koran vs Genesis. *Creation 24*(2), 46-51. Retrieved from https://creation.com/the-koran-quran-vs-genesis

References

Creation Stories. (n.d.). Retried September 14, 2019 from http://www.historyworld.net/wrldhis/PlainTextHistories.asp?historyid=ab83

Dapice, A. (2006). The Medicine Wheel. *Journal of Transcultural Nursing, 17*(3), 251-260. doi: 10.1177/1043659606288383

De Rios, M. & Winkelman, M. (2018). Shamanism and Altered States of Consciousness: An Introduction. *Journal of Psychoactive Drugs, 21*(1), 1-7, doi: 10.1080/02791072.1989.10472137

De Velasco, F. (2005). Descent into the Underworld. In Jones, L., Eliade, M., & Adams, C. (Eds.), *Encyclopedia of Religion* (2nd ed.). Detroit, MI: Thomson Gale.

Evans, A. (2019). *Trance Dance of the San.* Retrieved from https://www.thoughtco.com/what-is-the-trance-dance-44077

Gleissner, G. (2017). *What Is Dance Movement Therapy?* Retrieved from https://www.psychologytoday.com/intl/blog/hope-eating-disorder-recovery/201704/what-is-dance-movement-therapy

Halvorson, H. & Kragh, H. (2017). *Cosmology and Theology.* Retrieved September 17, 2019 from https://plato.stanford.edu/entries/cosmology-theology/#1

Harvey, G. & Wallis, R. (2016). *Historical Dictionary of Shamanism* (2nd ed.). Lanham, MD: Rowman & Littlefield.

Hoppál, M. (2013). *Shamans and Symbols.* Budapest, Central Hungary: International Society for Shamanistic Research.

Krippner, S. (2007). Humanity's First Healers: Psychological and Psychiatric Stances on Shamans and Shamanism. *Revista de Psiquiatria Clínica 34*(1), 16-22., doi: 10.1590/S0101-60832007000700004

Lam, K. (2019). *Why Are Jason Momoa and Other Native Hawaiians Protesting a Telescope on Mauna Kea? What's at Stake?* Retrieved September 18, 2019 from https://www.usatoday.com/story/news/nation/2019/08/21/mauna-kea-tmt-protests-hawaii-native-rights-telescope/1993037001/

References

Laufer, B. (1917). Origin of the Word Shaman. *American Anthropologist, 19*(3), 361-371. Retrieved from http://www.jstor.org/stable/660223

Leeming, D. (2010). *Creation Myths of the World: An Encyclopedia.* Santa Barbara, CA: ABC-CLIO.

Luna, L. (2003). *Ayahuasca: Shamanism Shared Across Cultures.* Retrieved from https://www.culturalsurvival.org/publications/cultural-survival-quarterly/ayahuasca-shamanism-shared-across-cultures

Mackinnon, C. (2018). Shamanism Made Easy: Awaken and Develop the Shamanic Force Within. Carlsbad, CA: Hay House, Inc.

Mash, S. Kovera, C., Buck, B., Norenberg, M., Shapshak, P., Hearn, W., & Sanchez-Ramos, J. (1998). Medication Development of Ibogaine as a Pharmacotherapy for Drug Dependence. *Annals of the New York Academy of Sciences, 844*(1), 274-292, doi: 10.1111/j.1749-6632.1998.tb08242.x

McCann, C. (n.d.) *Eight Crystals for Better Energy.* Retrieved from https://goop.com/wellness/spirituality/the-8-essential-crystals/

McGee, K. (2019). *How to Identify Liberty Cap Mushrooms.* Retrieved from https://www.hunker.com/13427787/how-to-identify-liberty-cap-mushrooms

Medicine Wheel. (2018). Retrieved September 7, 2019 from https://www.newworldencyclopedia.org/entry/Medicine_wheel

Morejón, J. (2018). From the *Areito to the Cordon:* Indigenous Healing Dances. *Revista Brasileira de Estudos da Presença 8*(3), 563-591, doi: 10.1590/2237-266069826

National Aeronautics and Space Administration. (2019). *What is the Big Bang?* Retrieved September 18, 2019 from https://spaceplace.nasa.gov/big-bang/en/

Naranjo, C. (1974). The Healing Journey: New Approaches to Consciousness. New York, NY: Pantheon Books.

References

Nicholas, L. & Ogame, K. (2006). Psilocybin Mushroom Handbook: Easy Indoor & Outdoor Cultivation. Oakland, CA: Ed Rosenthal.

Papadimitropoulos, P. (2009). Psychedelic Trance: Ritual, Belief and Transcendental Experience in Modern Raves. *Durham Anthropology Journal, 16*(2), 6-74. ISSN:1742-2930.

Pedrosa, K., Lucena, C., De Lucena, R., & Lopes, S. (2018). Traditional Techniques for the Management of Cactaceae in the Americas: The Relationship Between Use and Conservation. *Ethnobiology Letters 9*(2), 276-282, doi: 10.14237/ebl.9.2.2018.1117

Pelikan, J. (1987). Christianity: Christianity in Western Europe. In Jones, L., Eliade, M., & Adams, C. (Eds.), *Encyclopedia of Religion* (2nd ed.). Detroit, MI: Thomson Gale.

Pentikäinen, J. The Shamanic Drum as Cognitive Map. *Cahiers de Littérature Orale, 67-68*. Retrieved from https://journals.openedition.org/clo/445?lang=en

Perry, P. (2018). *The Environmental Cost of Fast Fashion*. Retrieved September 18, 2019 from https://www.independent.co.uk/life-style/fashion/environment-costs-fast-fashion-pollution-waste-sustainability-a8139386.html

Pinchbeck, D. (2002). A Psychedelic Journey into the Heart of Contemporary Shamanism. New York, NY: Broadway Books.

Rasmussen, S. (2004). "Magic," Power, and Ritual in Shamanism. In Walter, M. & Fridman, E. (Eds.), *Shamanism: An Encyclopedia of World Beliefs, Practices, and Culture, Volume 1* (pp. 161-167). Santa Barbara, CA: ABC-CLIO.

Redd, N. (2017). *What is Cosmology? Definition & History*. Retrieved September 17, 2019 from https://www.space.com/16042-cosmology.html

Rosen, D. (2009). *Why We Dream, and What Happens When We Do*. Retrieved from https://www.psychologytoday.com/intl/blog/sleeping-angels/200905/why-we-dream-and-what-happens-when-we-do

References

Schultes, R., Hofmann, A., & Ratsch, C. (2001). *Plants of the Gods: Their Sacred, Healing, and Hallucinogenic Powers* (2nd ed.) New York, NY: Healing Arts Press.

Serr, S. (2019a). Shamanic Middle World Spirits: Risks, Empowerment, and Safety. Retrieved from http://www.shamanism-101.com/Middle_World_Spirits.html

Serr, S. (2019b). Shamanism and the Upper World. Retrieved from http://www.shamanism-101.com/Shamanism_Upper_World.html

Serr, S. (2019c). *The Shamanic World: Power Animals and Nature*. Retrieved from http://www.shamanism-101.com/Shamanism_Lower_World.html

"Shamanistic Dance, Purposeful Ecstacy." (n.d.) Retrieved September 17, 2019 from https://disco.teak.fi/asia/shamanistic-dance-purposeful-ecstasy/

Siikala, A. (1987). Descent into the Underworld. In Jones, L., Eliade, M., & Adams, C. (Eds.), *Encyclopedia of Religion* (2nd ed.). Detroit, MI: Thomson Gale.

Sullivan, Z. (2019). *The Real Reason the Amazon Is on Fire*. Retrieved September 18, 2019 from https://time.com/5661162/why-the-amazon-is-on-fire/

Sumegi, A. (2008). *Dreamworlds of Shamanism and Tibetan Buddhism*. Albany, NY: State University of New York Press.

The International Union for Conservation of Nature and Natural Resources. (2017). *Echinopsis pachanoi*. Gland, Vaud: Ostalaza, C., Cáceres, F., & Roque, J.

The International Union for Conservation of Nature and Natural Resources. (2017). *Lophophora williamsii*. Gland, Vaud: Terry, M.

The Inuit. (n.d). Retrieved September 17, 2019 from https://firstpeoplesofcanada.com/fp_groups/fp_inuit5.html

Third Wave, Co. (n.d.a). *The Essential Guide to Ayahuasca*. Retrieved September 14, 2019 from https://thethirdwave.co/psychedelics/ayahuasca/#history--stats

Third Wave, Co. (n.d.b) *What is the Legality of Ayahuasca in*

References

Your Home Country? Retrieved September 14, 2019 from https://thethirdwave.co/legality-ayahuasca/

Tributsch, H. Shamanic Trance Journey with Animal Spirits: Ancient "Scientific" Strategy Dealing with Inverted Otherworld. *Advances in Anthropology, 8*(3), 91-126. doi: 10.4236/aa.2018.83006

Turner, E. (2004). Shamanism and Spirit. *Expedition Magazine, 46*(1), 12-15. Retrieved from https://www.penn.museum/sites/expedition/shamanism-and-spirit/

Walsh, R. (1994). The Making of a Shaman: Calling, Training, and Culmination. *Journal of Humanistic Psychology, 34*(3), 7-30, doi: 10.1177/00221678940343003

Walsh, R. (2001). Shamanic Experiences: A Developmental Analysis. *Journal of Humanistic Psychology, 41*(3), 31-52, doi: 10.1177/0022167801413004

Walsh, R. (2014). The World of Shamanism: New Views of an Ancient Tradition. Woodbury, MN: Llewellyn Worldwide.

Warber, S., Bruyere, R., Weintrub, K., & Dieppe, P. (2015). A Consideration of the Perspectives of Healing Practitioners on Research into Energy Healing. *Global Advances in Health and Medicine, 4*(Suppl), 72-78, doi: 10.7453/gahmj.2015.014.suppl

Winkelman, M. (2010). Shamanism: A Biopsychosocial Paradigm of Consciousness and Healing. Santa Barbara, CA: ABC-CLIO.

World Ocean Network. (n.d.). *Land-based pollution (Wate, Sewage Water, Coastal Development Activities, Inland Activities...).* Retrieved September 18, 2019 from https://www.worldoceannetwork.org/won-part-6/carem-wod-2014-4/thematic-resources-pollution/facts-figures-pollution/

About the Author

Monique Joiner Siedlak is a writer, witch, and warrior on a mission to awaken people to their greatest potential through the power of storytelling infused with mysticism, modern paganism, and new age spirituality. At the young age of 12, she began rigorously studying the fascinating philosophy of Wicca. By the time she was 20, she was self-initiated into the craft, and hasn't looked back ever since. To this day, she has authored over 40 books pertaining to the magick and mysteries of life.

To find out more about Monique Joiner Siedlak artistically, spiritually, and personally, feel free to visit her **official website**.

www.mojosiedlak.com

facebook.com/mojosiedlak
x.com/mojosiedlak
instagram.com/mojosiedlak
pinterest.com/mojosiedlak
bookbub.com/authors/monique-joiner-siedlak

More Books by Monique

African Spirituality Beliefs and Practices

Hoodoo
- Seven African Powers: The Orishas
- Cooking for the Orishas
- Lucumi: The Ways of Santeria
- Voodoo of Louisiana
- Haitian Vodou
- Orishas of Trinidad
- Connecting with your Ancestors
- Blood Magick
- The Orishas
- Vodun: West Africa's Spiritual Life
- Marie Laveau: Life of a Voodoo Queen
- Candomblé: Dancing for the God
- Umbanda
- Exploring the Rich and Diverse World

Divination Magic for Beginners
- Divination with Runes
- Divination with Diloggún

More Books by Monique

Divination with Osteomancy
Divination with the Tarot
Divination with Stones

The Beginner's Guide to Inner Growth
Astral Projection for Beginners
Meditation for Beginners
Reiki for Beginners

Mastering Your Inner Potential
Creative Visualization
Manifesting With the Law of Attraction

Holistic Healing and Energy
Healing Animals with Reiki
Crystal Healing
Communicating with Your Spirit Guides

Empathic Understanding and Enlightenment
Being an Empath Today

Life on Fire
Healing Your Inner Child
Change Your Life
Raising Your Vibe

The Indie Author's Guides
The Indie Author's Guide to Fast Drafting Your Novel

Get a Handle on Life
Get a Handle on Stress
Time Bound
Get a Handle on Anxiety
Get a Handle on Depression
Get a Handle on Procrastination

More Books by Monique

The Holistic Yoga and Wellness Series
Yoga for Beginners
Yoga for Stress
Yoga for Back Pain
Yoga for Weight Loss
Yoga for Flexibility
Yoga for Advanced Beginners
Yoga for Fitness
Yoga for Runners
Yoga for Energy
Yoga for Your Sex Life
Yoga to Beat Depression and Anxiety
Yoga for Menstruation
Yoga to Detox Your Body
Yoga to Tone Your Body

The DIY Body Care Series
Creating Your Own Body Butter
Creating Your Own Body Scrub
Creating Your Own Body Spray

SUPPORT ME BY LEAVING A REVIEW!

www.ingramcontent.com/pod-product-compliance
Lightning Source LLC
Chambersburg PA
CBHW060835050426
42453CB00008B/696